ANCIENT ROCK CARVINGS
OF THE CENTRAL SIERRA:
THE NORTH FORK INDIAN
PETROGLYPHS

ANCIENT ROCK CARVINGS

OF THE CENTRAL SIERRA:

THE NORTH FORK INDIAN

PETROGLYPHS

Willis A. Gortner

PORTOLA PRESS
P.O. Box 620361
Woodside, California 94062

To Susan

    For her patience, her helpfulness, her support, her understanding of my petroglyphing lifestyle.

CONTENTS

FOREWORD...xv

I. WHY ANOTHER BOOK ON PETROGLYPHS?.......................1

II. WHY ARE THESE CARVINGS CALLED PETROGLYPHS?...........3

III. HOW WERE THE PETROGLYPHS MADE?......................4

    Why are few artifact tools--or none--associ-
    ated with the carving of petroglyphs?...........5

IV. WHO MADE THESE PETROGLYPHS?..........................6

    Which Indian tribes are associated with lands
    bordering the petroglyphs?......................6

    What clues may be provided from the material
    and social culture of these tribes?.............7

V. HOW ANCIENT ARE THE PETROGLYPHS?.....................10

    What ways have been used successfully in
    dating an occasional petroglyph panel in
    the West or Southwest?.........................10

        a) Weathering and patination..................10

        b) Tribal history or legends..................11

        c) Superposition of symbols...................11

        d) Appearance of historical figures...........11

        e) Radiocarbon dating of campsites and
           archaeological deposits.............12

        f) Geological deposits........................12

        g) Dating by the styles and symbols of
           the petroglyphs....................13

        h) The use of Indian artifacts................13

Can the projectile point style and size be related to a particular period?.................14

What is known about the projectile points that are found along the North Fork of the American River?..........................16

How do the Cedars projectile points relate to other prehistoric artifacts?...................18

What do these artifacts tell us about the age of the petroglyphs along the North Fork?.......25

If the petroglyphs are thousands of years old, why do some now appear to be rapidly disappearing?................................26

VI. WHERE ARE THE PETROGLYPHS FOUND?...................29

Were the North Fork petroglyph sites known previously?..............................31

Where should one look to find such petroglyphs?..............................32

Do these criteria for a petroglyph site differ from other areas where petroglyphs are found?...........................33

Are the petroglyphs near identifiable Indian campsites?....................................33

Are the petroglyph sites also game ambush sites?..35

Are basalt quarries near the petroglyphs?.........35

VII. WHAT TYPES OF SYMBOLS ARE FOUND IN THE CARVINGS?...................................36

Classification of the symbols into "elements".......36

Distribution of the symbols at different sites...42

Do these petroglyphs conform to a particular "style"?...................................45

VIII. WHY WERE THE PETROGLYPHS MADE?.................50

   Are they intended for communicating some
   message?..50

   Why do some sites have many symbols, others
   only a few, and many have none?.................51

   Is there evidence of more than one group
   making the petroglyphs?.........................53

IX. WHAT DO THE PETROGLYPH SYMBOLS MEAN?.............56

   What might the early Indian wish to record?........56

      a] A record of astronomical events or
         observations............................56

      b] A record of environmental events...........57

      c] A count, such as a recording of
         passage of time.........................58

      d] A recording of a geographical area; a
         map.....................................58

      e] A record of a personal or cultural
         nature..................................65

      f] A record of religious or magic or
         ceremonial significance.................67

      g] Instructions, perhaps via Indian sign
         language................................73

   Can even the simple symbols that occur
   frequently be interpreted?......................73

X. DO THE PETROGLYPHS BY THE NORTH FORK CHANGE
ANY EXISTING THEORIES?..............................78

XI. WHERE HAS ALL THIS BROUGHT US?..................80

APPENDICES...82

    Appendix A-Recording the North Fork petroglyphs....82

    Appendix B-The North Fork petroglyphs in
        detailed sketches.............................83

PUBLICATIONS CITED..180

INDEX...182

FIGURES

Scheme Used for Classifying Projectile Points............17

Some of the Basalt Projectile Points Found
    at the Cedars.......................................22

Distribution of Martis Complex Sites Known in 1960.......24

North Fork Indian Petroglyph Sites......................30

Some Examples of the Use of Basalt Inclusions in
    Petroglyph Symbols.................................34

Which of These is Properly Categorized as a RAKE?........38

Which of These is Properly Categorized as a SUN DISC?....39

Which of These is Properly Categorized as a PAW?........40

Rakes with Wavy, Parallel Lines.........................46

Some Unusual Symbols at Site #2 near Wabena..............54

Similar Symbols with Looping Lines......................54

Map #1?...60

Map #2?...61

Map #3?...63

Map #4?...64

Map #5?...66

Possible Shaman Symbols in the Rock at Site #27.........69

Wavy or Curved Lines in Symbols and Numbering Four.......71

"Circles" with Crosses as Symbols......................72

Possible Supernatural Beings or Thunderbirds............74

Comparison of Symbols at Site #2 with One in
    Ventura County....................................75

TABLES

Type Classification of Projectile Points in Three
    Major Collections at the Cedars......................19

A Comparison of the Relative Distribution of
    Projectile Points at Martis Sites and Those
    at the North Fork Sites.............................23

Design Elements Used in Petroglyph Classification
    by Heizer and Baumhoff..............................37

Comparison of Symbols at Major Petroglyph Sites
    and Near Campgrounds along the North Fork...........44

Style Characteristics and Suggested Dating...............47

FOREWORD

The field research on the North Fork petroglyphs began in the early 1970's, but became a full-fledged annual summer program in 1978. Each year has seen the addition of many new sites. Nearly all of these sites have been revisited, sometimes several times over the years--and new symbols frequently have been noted long after the original finding, for many are very faint and badly weathered.

Though a few elusive sites mentioned to me by friends have not yet been found and recorded, it seems time to make this progress report. It adds some new and provocative findings to our limited knowledge of the prehistory of the Central Sierra.

It is not coincidental that this work unfolds in the manner of a detective story.

Even the amateur archaeologist needs and uses some of the talents of the detective. Both seek elusive clues from a variety of sources, often far afield. The fragmentary clues are finally brought together, sometimes one clarifying or reinforcing the other, until a picture emerges. Sometimes a murky picture, but at any rate a step or two further in one's knowledge.

And the detective and the archaeologist [the prehistory detective] try to find answers to who, when, where, what, why.

So read this as an archaeological detective story. It will take the reader, as it took me, through the fragmentary clues which finally arrive at some fairly clear answers of "who, when, where, what" for ancient rock carvings in the Central Sierra Nevada. Some educated guesses are even suggested for the "why" of these records in stone by prehistoric man.

I. WHY ANOTHER BOOK ON PETROGLYPHS?

In recent years, many questions have been posed to me by friends and fellow Sierra buffs sharing my interest and curiosity in the ancient Indian rock carvings called petroglyphs, a unique aspect of the Indian's culture. And I've asked myself these same questions--How and why and when were they made? Where are they, and what do they mean?

The semi-wilderness regions in California adjacent to the upper reaches of the North Fork of the American River, above the Royal Gorge, can offer a fascinating experience to one who may have some degree of interest in the early Indians who roamed this area of the Central Sierra Nevada mountains. The lands around the North Fork and its tributory streams and creeks will interest some because of the ancient Indian migratory trail that paralled the river and went on over the Sierra crest toward Lake Tahoe and Squaw Valley. Others will be interested in the hundreds of spearheads, dart points, and arrowheads found in this area. And others, including myself, will find enjoyment in examining and even discovering the ancient Indian rock carvings that are present in surprising abundance in lands abutting the North Fork. At least some discussion in this little volume will touch on each of these interests, because they all may help us to some reasonable, albeit tentative, conclusions about the prehistoric Indians and this rock art form they had.

There are a number of books that have been written specifically on Indian petroglyphs. Three major undertakings are those by Mallery [1,* "Picture-Writing of the American Indians"], originally published in 1889; by Heizer and Baumhoff [2, "Prehistoric Rock Art of Nevada and Eastern California"], published in 1962; and the extension of this in the book by Heizer and Clewlow [3,"Prehistoric Rock Art of California"], which appeared in 1973. Yet these major treatises still answer few of the many questions which people ask about these petroglyphs. One reason is that mentioned by Heizer and Clewlow [3]:

We have...reached the point where general characterization can lead us to no new insights. The time has come when only detailed regional studies, based upon all available information, will lead to deeper understanding of the rock art styles, their chronology, and perhaps their functions.

The present volume is recording what may be the first intensive, detailed regional study of California petroglyphs.

---

*The underlined figures cite literature references listed at the back of this book [p. ~~175~~ 180].

1

It may be particularly timely because, as Heizer and Clewlow noted, scant attention has been directed to the petroglyphs in the Central Sierra region; they expressed the hope that their limited efforts would serve to call attention to an area that had been unduly neglected.

The semi-wilderness lands bordering the upper reaches of the North Fork of the American River particularly have been over-looked because essentially all of the land is privately held, is posted and patrolled against trespassing, so that access to the public is not available. I have been fortunate in that I am a member of the major land-holder, the North Fork Association [The Cedars], and thus have had access to the area where the petroglyphs in this study are to be found.

The studies continue. But adequate information has now been accumulated to help answer some of the many questions, and to formulate some tentative hypotheses or explanations from the clues provided.

II. WHY ARE THESE CARVINGS CALLED PETROGLYPHS?

These carvings are inscriptions on a rock. From the Greek, the word "petro" means a rock; we see it used when we refer to "petrified" wood. The other part of the word, "glyph", relates to the Greek word for a carving. Both petroglyph and hieroglyph relate to carved or incised figures, characters, or symbols. But a hieroglyph may be on various materials, such as clay, while a petroglyph is only on rock.

Sometimes the literature refers to rock art, and of course, that refers not only to rock carving but also rock painting. The ancient Indian rock carvings along the tributaries of the North Fork of the American River are appropriately called "petroglyphs"; that is, figures or symbols [glyphs] that have been pecked, scratched, carved, or otherwise engraved on the surface of a rock.

III. HOW WERE THE PETROGLYPHS MADE?

There are numerous pitted, broken, or badly scarred rocks or outcroppings along the North Fork of the American River that are unsuitable for petroglyphs. The smoothly glaciated granite and basaltic rocks are by far the best, and are where the petroglyphs may be found. Grant observes [4] that

> there are great concentrations of petroglyphs pecked shallowly into the dark brown or black patinated surfaces of basaltic rocks in that part of California that drains into the Great Basin. The pecking stone, breaking through the patina or "desert varnish" to the lighter original rock color, leaves an image of high contrast that will remain fresh-looking for many hundreds of years.

The North Fork petroglyphs are all found as carvings in granite or basalt, both being igneous rocks. Granite is particularly rich in alkaline feldspar and quartz, the hardness of which is about 6-8 on a hardness scale where talc is 1 and a diamond is 10. Quartz and obsidian should be able to scratch these igneous rocks, but the glassy obsidian will tend to shatter or dull quickly. [It also is not available in this region, and certainly would not have been used in the rock carving.]

Some of the petroglyph symbols are very fine and wavy [see p. 45], with many wavy lines close to each other and parallel to each other. It is likely that the carvings were largely made by a pecking process; indeed, some clearly show the individual pits or depressions of the pecking process. The grooves may then have been scratched smoother, and sand might be used in the groove to help smooth the incision.

Even in granite, with a rather coarse texture of mineral elements, scratching a symbol is not an easy or rapid process. I attempted this with both quartz and obsidian tools, and after a half-hour had a barely discernible symbol [a simple circle] in the pink-encrusted granite rock. Pecking would be a more satisfactory and likely mechanism.

Some years ago Busby et al [5] reported on their efforts to manufacture petroglyphs by pecking as well as scratching methods, and using granite as a pecking tool raw material. They found that pecking a "tailed circle" in granite required 40 minutes; a "rectilinear grid" took them 27 minutes when they made the symbol in granite and the pecking tool was either basalt or granite, with a hardness of 6-8. A more complicated "horned lizard" symbol took 115 minutes to completion [nearly 15,000 blows at 126 per minute]. A "circle with two tails" required 44 minutes of pecking, but putting a scratched cross-hatching pattern on it only took about 5 minutes; however, they noted that the scratched designs were quite shallow. Finally, this semi-scientific study under field conditions showed that the patinated or crusty surface is much easier to penetrate than the interior under that crust [perhaps 3-4 versus 6-8 in the hardness scale]. Very few of the North Fork petroglyphs now penetrate much beyond the weathered surface crust of granite, but those at the site near Wabena Creek [Site #2, see p. 30] clearly do.

<u>Why are few artifact tools--or none--associated with the carving of petroglyphs?</u> The Indians who made these petroglyphs were from a stone-age culture. Sharp rocks would have been used in making the incisions in the granite or the basalt. In no instance, however, is there any evidence that a special rock, or a flaked type of rock, was used to make the symbols. If a special type of tool was used, any broken during the carving of the petroglyphs should have been around or by the site. None has been found. Indeed, there is no evidence that a special hammering or carving tool was used at any of the many hundreds of petroglyph sites known in the Western states. Heizer and Baumhoff [2] reported that at some of the major petroglyph sites which they examined, great numbers of hammerstones must have been used, but in no case was any worked tool found near the petroglyphs.

Apparently, the Indians merely used suitable hard rocks found in the area, and these were discarded after use or when they became dull. It is unfortunate, in a way, because a worked artifact might be used to tell us something about the people making the petroglyph and thus also might be used as a dating mechanism for the petroglyph.

IV. WHO MADE THESE PETROGLYPHS?

The petroglyphs were not made by the Indians occupying these lands when the White man came to California, but presumably were made by their ancestors.

Which Indian tribes are associated with lands bordering the petroglyphs? Three tribes lived around the Central Sierra Nevada range during historic times. The Washo is the Indian tribe on the eastern side of the Sierra crest and in the desert area of Western Nevada near Carson City and Reno, as well as along the Truckee River and the shores of Lake Tahoe. The Washo have been considered an offshoot of the Paiute Indians in the Great Basin area. [The Great Basin is largely a desert area that extends from the Colorado plateau on the east to the Sierra Nevada range on the west.]

The Southern Maidu tribe [the Nisenan] occupied the foothills and mountainous regions around Northeastern California between Sacramento and the Feather River. Wilson and Towne [9] consider this tribe as having occupied the drainage areas of the Yuba, Bear, and American Rivers, including the lower drainages of the Feather River.

The third tribal group, the Miwok Indians, has been called the true foothill people, and lived further south in the regions of the Central Sierra including Yosemite Valley.

These Indians, then, are the modern day tribes whose ancestors are most likely to have made the petroglyphs along the North Fork of the American River. The historic boundaries of these tribes came together near the Sierra crest and around the passes leading to Lake Tahoe.

One should not discount the possibility that the Washo tribe may be descendants of the Indians first inhabiting [during the summers] the North Fork valley. As will be discussed later [see p. 21], the peoples of the "Martis Complex" were likely responsible for carving the petroglyphs. This tribal group clearly occupied lands on both sides of the Sierras. Elsasser [7] says:

> The dilema of the northern Sierra Nevada, in sum, is not concerned with the derivation of the Martis people; their roots seem to lie in the Great Basin. If they crossed the Sierra Nevada about 1000 B.C., they could have represented another wave of migrants from the Great Basin to Central California.

Elston [8] concluded that the Martis Complex derived from a Great Basin-oriented culture and that the Martis peoples were direct ancestors of the historic Washo based in Nevada; later he expressed some doubts of this [23].

The Indian tribe in historic times most commonly associated with the lands around the North Fork of the American River [as well as the Yuba and Bear Rivers] is the Southern Maidu, or Nisenan. On the south their territory met up with the Miwok between the American River and the Cosumnes River. The Nisenan were called "Diggers" by the early Whites in California, but these Indians were hunters as well, having communal deer drives and winter hunts for the black bear.

What clues may be provided from the material and social culture of these tribes? The winters in the Sierra are so severe and snowy as to prevent permanent occupancy by the aborigines, but the Indians used this mountainous area for big game hunting during the summer months. If they came from the foothills, the culture there might relate to their practise of pecking petroglyphs in the Sierra.

Several writers have observed that the modern-day concept of an "Indian tribe" derives from an attempt to make an ethnographic classification, but is not the reality of many of the peoples. Generally, there was no "Indian nation" as such. Rather, both the Nisenan and Miwok centered their social and political units in village "tribelets".

The Hill Nisenan had limited contact beyond their village centers. However, they were known to have trade with other tribes; Wilson and Towne [9] noted that the Nisenan traded such things as acorns and shells with the Washo for dried fish from Pyramid Lake, and that trade also brought into the area such useful minerals as steatite [soapstone] and obsidian.

Some of the family and tribal beliefs and customs of these Indians are worth noting because they may give at least a little insight into the significance or meaning of the symbols in the petroglyphs along the North Fork. Among primitive tribes it was common to divide into a system of social units such as "clans" [a unit larger than the family but claiming descent from a common ancestor--the family geneology] and "moieties" [two complementary halves or tribal subdivisions, not heritary; indeed, a person of one moiety generally could only marry one of the other moiety, thus helping avoid in-breeding of the tribe].

These tribal groups often used "totems", objects or symbols, to distinguish their clan, moiety, or tribe. Such emblems are seen in totem poles, for example.

Kroeber [4] mentions that

...among all the Sierra Miwok, clans have wholly dis-
appeared. The exogamous moiety however remains, and its
totemic aspects are rather more developed than in the

south. The Miwok carry the totemic scheme farthest, dividing the universe as it were into totemic halves, so that all its natural contents are potential totems of one or the other moiety....Among the Miwok the personal name refers to an animal or object of the individual's moiety, but the totem itself is hardly ever expressed in the name.

Conrotto amplifies on this [10], saying of these moieties,

Its people were divided into land and water...The land-side was made up of these totems: bear, puma, wild cat, dog, fox, racoon, tree squirrel, badger, jack rabbit, eagle, condor...sky, sun, stars, night, fire, earth, salt, bow, arrows...The water side consisted of deer, antelope, coyote, beaver, otter, buzzard...salamander, water snake...cloud, rain, fog, water, lake, ice, mud, lightning, rock...

In historic times, the Sierra Miwok in their ritual dances identified their moiety by painting their faces and bodies [27], the land moiety using horizontal stripes and the water moiety by spots [a totem presumed to represent the spots of fawns].

It is of interest that Mallery [1] nearly a hundred years ago wrote [regarding petroglyphs in Idaho] that some of the petroglyph symbols appear to be totemic characters, and might have been made to record the names of Indians passing there. One wonders whether some symbols in North Fork petroglyphs may represent totems for one of the moieties as listed above.

There were several kinds of shaman or tribal priest-doctor among California Indians, including the Maidu [Nisenan] and Miwok. They included the bear shaman, rattlesnake shaman, and the rain or weather shaman. The shaman doctors were considered to have supernatural powers, often associated with particular specialties. Kroeber's article discusses three of these shamans associated with one of these specialties [4]:

The rain doctor seems generally to have exercised his control over the weather in addition to possessing the abilities of an ordinary shaman...
        The rattlesnake doctor...business of course was to cure snake bites; in some cases also to prevent them...There appears to have been some inclination to regard the sun as the spirit to which rattlesnake doctors particularly looked...
        The bear doctor was recognized over the entire state...Generally bear shamans were thought invulnerable, or at least to possess the power of returning to life. They inspired an extraordinary fear and yet seem to have been encouraged...Naturally enough, their power

was considered to be derived from bears, particularly the grizzly. It is the ferocity and tenacity of this species that clearly impressed the imagination of the Indians, and a more accurately descriptive name of the caste would be grizzly-bear shamans.

One more piece of information may be useful. For the Miwok, four is a sacred or ritual number. For the Nisenan, the ritual number is five. [Many other California tribes have five or other numbers as significant in ritualistic symbolism.]

V. HOW ANCIENT ARE THE PETROGLYPHS?

Except for unusual circumstances, the times when the petroglyphs were carved in the rocks will necessarily be quite uncertain. Nevertheless, there are a number of ways for inferring the time when some of the rock carvings were made.

What ways have been used successfully in dating an occasional petroglyph panel in the West or Southwest? Many of the following methods are not suitable for the North Fork petroglyphs, but a few are.

a) **Weathering and patination** of the rock may provide a clue. In desert areas of the Great Basin, a coating of so-called "desert varnish" is found on rocks, and this may have a different thickness in the petroglyphs pecked or scratched on them. This desert varnish is a type of weathering that takes a long time to appear. The amount of varnish coating and the time required for development of the varnish can be used to make a rough estimate of when the petroglyph may have been incised. In the Sierra, however, this type of coating doesn't appear, and there is no possibility of using this method.

Even a weathering of the petroglyph symbols on the rock from exposure to many seasons offers limited opportunity; the degree of exposure to weathering will depend so much on the winter weather conditions, the rainfall, possible flooding, exposure to strong winds and dust or sand, and the orientation of the petroglyph on the rock. For example, a petroglyph that is at an angle on the rock might be gradually abraded by sliding snow and ice, in contrast to one that is on a flat, horizontal outcropping.

Yet there is some hope of this method of getting at the age of the petroglyph. While the rocks in the Sierra do not have the "desert varnish", the granite outcroppings frequently do show a surface discoloration, pinkish in color, that gives the marked contrast for the petroglyph carving that has penetrated only a few millimeters deep, thus exposing the lighter colored granite bedrock. Over the millenia when the original glaciated granite was exposed to rainwater, water soaked into the minutely porous rock; later the seepage was gradually brought up to the surface by capillarity and evaporation. Over the years, this leached or removed some soluble alkaline salts from the rock and thus increased the porosity and formed a crust to the depth the water had penetrated. It left on the surface crust some of the reddish iron oxides which the water had brought up from minerals within the granite.

It was interesting to see the extent to which the rust-colored iron-rich surface layer had regenerated in the incised lines during the ninety-odd years since modern human graffiti was

10

carved [and precisely dated] in the petroglyph panel rocks at Site #27 [p. 30]. At this site in the 1880's, the Mark Hopkins "Summit Soda Springs Hotel" was a popular summer resort reached by stage coach from the railroad near Donner Summit. Patrons of the hotel frequently carved their names or initials and the date in the granite outcropping by the river where major Indian petroglyph carvings occur. Even now, the 90-year old ["modern"] lines in the granite appear to be freshly carved. They show no evidence of a return of the pink surface stain. By contrast, the immediately adjacent but much more ancient Indian rock carvings appear consistently weathered with a dull stain re-appearing in the incised lines, though not nearly approaching the depth of color of the pink crust of the granite bedrock itself. Obviously, the petroglyphs at this site were many hundreds of years older than the "modern" carvings made alongside of them nearly a century ago. A more detailed, geochemical study here might offer a crude time scale for the much older Indian carvings.

   b) **Tribal history or legends** might provide a clue to the time of origin of a petroglyph. There are many evidences that this is not a productive pathway. Mallery [1] observed that numerous petroglyphs occur along the Truckee River and near Verdi and Reno, a region that had been the home of the Washo Indians for centuries. He noted that none of the Indians still there knew anything of these petroglyphs; when one who was said to be over a hundred years old was taken to them, he commented that when he was only a few years old, they appeared then as they do now. And Mallery quoted this in 1883, a century ago.

   Heizer and Baumhoff [2] mention that

      there seems to be no unambiguous record of Indians claiming to have made pecked petroglyphs.

Their origin and meaning are lost in antiquity, and did not remain in their tribal legends.

   c) **Superposition of symbols** on a petroglyph might give some clue, at least as to which symbols and styles might be the oldest. This superposition has been noted in some petroglyphs elsewhere in the California and Nevada regions, but does not seem to be present in the petroglyphs along the North Fork of the American River.

   d) **Appearance of historical figures** sometimes can be helpful when the symbols clearly are recognizable as things in historical times. Some petroglyphs in the West and Southwest have horses, Spanish conquistadores, pack trains, guns, and other things that can be associated with known history of the past few hundred years. No such symbols have been seen on the petroglyphs along the North Fork. Most likely this lack may suggest a far greater, prehistoric antiquity of the rock carving.

e) **Radiocarbon dating of campsites and archaeological deposits** near the petroglyphs. Where there are "midden deposits", accumulated organic matter from human occupation of a site, there is a possibility of using carbon-14 radiochemical dating of the site. Usually this is possible in very dry areas or in caves suitable for habitation. The areas in the Sierra, however, are only temporary summer hunting grounds and offer neither suitable caves to protect from moisture nor long-term occupation by the Indians that might still retain wood or bone material that could be carbon-14 dated. Caves are rare in Nisenan territory, especially any showing occupation [9].

Charcoal is more persistant than organic matter, and may remain for many centuries. This radiocarbon method has been used in drier areas to help date a particular site and, by cross-dating, to relate to petroglyphs even at another site.

In the Martis Valley near Truckee a pitted petroglyph [designated Pla-5 site, ref. 2] was found in association with a midden deposit containing stone artifacts; the tentative dating of the site occupation [though not by radiocarbon analysis] was somewhere between 1000 B.C. and 500 A.D. An earlier age was suggested by two radiocarbon dates made on an obviously related "Martis Complex" site perhaps 20 miles away at Spooner Lake in Nevada, across the lake from the Homewood resort and about 3 miles east of Lake Tahoe [8]. The C-14 date of about 5100 B.C. from one charcoal sample in the excavations there suggests that the early Martis peoples or their immediate ancestors may have existed [and carved petroglyphs] some 7000 years ago. However, the period of intensive occupation of the site was radiocarbon dated at somewhat before 1000 B.C., and was associated with a predominance of flaked stone artifacts similar to those in Martis Valley and identified with and characterizing the Martis Complex [see p. 23].

Another site near Lake Tahoe with Martis-type basalt projectile points was radiocarbon dated at 1340 B.C. [23]. Indeed, two earlier studies by Elston report Martis Complex dates of 1770 B.C. and 1530 B.C. at two different sites in Western Nevada, east of Lake Tahoe. And charcoal at a site at Squaw Valley with Martis-type points was dated at 2350 B.C. [23].

A Martis-type site near Auburn [a winter-spring village site, designated Pla-101] was dated at 1400 B.C. [11], and another near Oroville, California, had a carbon-14 date of 950 B.C. [Elsasser (7) states that the artifacts in the foothills near Oroville show affiliations with both the "Middle Central California Horizon" cultural sequence and the Martis Complex.]

f) **Geological deposits** may offer a dating clue. At one site in the West, a previously inhabited cave had been closed with pumice from a volcanic eruption; the petroglyph carvings within the cave thus had to have predated that eruption. Sometimes a flooding may have covered a carving with a deposit of gravel, and give some clue if the unusual environmental situation can be traced and dated. And sometimes the elevation or lowering of a lake can give dating information. In one area in Nevada the petroglyphs are on a cliff far above where a person could reach, and must have been made when the land under the petroglyphs had been much higher, presumably before a stream had been diverted to carry away the soil beneath the cliff. None of this, however, is useful for the Sierra petroglyph sites.

g) **Dating by the styles and symbols of the petroglyphs.** For the most part, this is the method commonly used by archaeologists in the West for assessing the age of petroglyph carvings. The types of symbols found and the interpretations of the various "styles" of these symbols for the North Fork petroglyphs will be discussed a little later [p. 36 et seq].

Heizer and Baumhoff [2] discuss dating of Nevada petroglyph styles of pecked and scratched carvings. They list four styles of carvings. They consider the Great Basin Representational style as dating from 1 A.D. to 1500 A.D. The Great Basin Rectilinear Abstract style also is inferred as running from 1A.D. to 1500 A.D. The Great Basin Curvilinear Abstract style is suggested as perhaps dating from 1000 B.C. to 1500 A.D. The most ancient of the petroglyph carving styles is called by them the Pit-and-Groove style, and has been ascribed to the period of 3000 and 5000 B.C. The pit-and-groove style is not commonly seen in the Sierras, however [though a pitted boulder has been reported in Martis Valley and in Sardine Valley north of Truckee].

Of the four classifications listed above, the style which the North Fork petroglyphs resemble the closest is the Great Basin Curvilinear Abstract; this is associated with the period of a thousand or so years before and after the birth of Christ. Clewlow [4] states that only the more recently designated Central Sierra style [see p. 48] is equivalent in antiquity and duration to the Great Basin petroglyphs.

h) **The use of Indian artifacts** associated with petroglyph sites may help date petroglyph carvings. This has not been used extensively by archaeologists interested in petroglyphs, but has been used in connection with other archaeological situations. There are many chipped knives, scrapers, awls and other flaked tools [all of basalt] found near the North Fork petroglyph sites or campgrounds. But the major artifacts that have been found are projectile points. [This term covers both arrowheads and the flaked and chipped stone artifacts such as spear or dart points, which preceded the bow and arrow.] The projectile points sometimes can be dated by other archaeological evidence [such as radiocarbon dating of charcoal associated with the artifacts in an excavation] and from this the petroglyphs near them can be said to be no older than the earliest projectile point there. The woods and mountains of the Sierra were used as hunting grounds, and it is completely unlikely that the petroglyphs were carved even before the early hunters appeared in the area around the North Fork of the American River. Obviously, later occupants might have made the petroglyphs, but they should have left artifacts of their presence. However, some of the evidence from other dating mechanisms described above might help one to resolve even this problem.

Thus, other than using the rather unsatisfactory 2500-year range suggested from dating of the petroglyph symbol styles, the use of projectile point types and their associated dates offers probably the best means of resolving the question, How ancient are these petroglyphs?

<u>Can the projectile point style and size be related to a particular period?</u> The answer seems to be yes. To get at this, it will be necessary to go over some of the prehistory of North American aborigines.

Several "cultures" are recognized by archaeologists in the West. The term "culture" is used to describe the occurrence of similar archaeological materials over a wide region [12]. It expresses the idea of similarity of a series of collections from a diverse area and thus implies a technology of peoples at that time and over that region. Two are of immediate concern here. One is the California Culture area, which covers much of the state west of the Sierra; and the other is the Great Basin Culture area, the desert-like area east of the Sierra and on to the Rockies.

The very ancient cultures in the Western United States have been termed the Llano, Folsom, and Plano Cultures. Radiocarbon dating indicates that these three followed each other and began some 12,000 years ago when there was an ice-free corridor extending down from Alaska and through Western Canada and to the Western states in the last big glaciation. This would thus be a time when the earliest inhabitants came down to the country from the Far North. The Plano culture ended some 7000 years ago, or about 5000 B.C.

A number of well-known and well-described projectile points are associated with these three early cultures. They include the Clovis fluted points, which are thin, some 3 to 6 inches long, about a fourth as wide as they are long, without "ears", and fluted toward the base end of the point; Folsom points, which are beautifully chipped, fluted on both sides nearly the whole length, are smaller than the Clovis points, a less lanceolate form, and with an indented base with "ears"; Plano points, which are leaf shaped, not fluted, and with a flat or concave base;

14

Sandia points, which are somewhat crudely chipped, have a rounded base or maybe a flat or indented base that might have been thinned by a short fluting, and with a well-developed shoulder on one edge; the Plainview point, which is like an unfluted Folsom point, with a square or concave base, parallel sides, and a strong median ridge from the chipping; the Eden point, which is well-made, long and slender, and with smooth, even chipping which may be chipped in flakes across the entire blade or from the edge to the median ridge, usually having a slightly square shoulder, making a stem and a squared base. Descriptions and numerous drawings of these projectile points are found in many books, including those by Macgowan [13], and especially Jennings [12].

The next period of archaeological cultures is the "Archaic Stage". It covers the period between 4000 and 7000 years ago, or 2000 to 5000 B.C. This stage includes the Topanga and Early California Cultures. There is considerable skepticism that the earliest cultures prior to the Archaic, such as the Folsom, extended into California, though there is no question that the cultures during the Archaic Stage were in California.

During this period a number of types of projectile points were used and identified at different sites in the West. Three are of immediate interest to us. The "Early Central California points" are leaf-shaped or stemmed, over 5 grams in weight and 4 centimeters long, roughly chipped, and of flint or slate [though most have been of obsidian at some sites near Sacramento]. The "Martis points" are mainly from basalt and with only a few from obsidian or chert, fairly large and heavy, roughly chipped, some shouldered [side-notched], fewer being tanged [barbed or end-notched], and bear some similarity to Pinto points. The "Pinto points" resemble Martis points, and have a stemmed or indented base.

As noted earlier [p. 12], the Martis Complex name derives from the site along the Martis Valley near Truckee, north of Lake Tahoe. The projectile points found there may have been only for spear or dart use. The leaf-shaped points generally exceed 2 inches in length. This also is when one first finds appreciable numbers of points with a contracting stem.

Jennings [12] notes that the archaeological evidence would place the Early Central California Culture at a period of 5000 to 3000 years before the present [3000-1000 B.C.], with the Martis Complex near the end of this period. Heizer and Baumhoff [2] and Elsasser [7] have placed the Martis Complex at 1000 B.C. to 500 A.D. [thus during the Middle Central California Culture]. A number of radiocarbon dates place the Martis Complex closer to 1500 B.C. [see p. 12].

Archaeological excavations of sites in the lower Sacramento

15

Valley region have included studies of artifacts and radiocarbon dating [2]. The "Early Horizon" layer among other things is characterized by large, heavy projectile points, with the dart or spear-thrower [atlatl] as the major weapon. The age for this "Early Horizon" deposit was somewhat over 4000 years old, or earlier than 2000 B.C.

The "Middle Horizon" [Middle Central California Culture] ranged from 2000 B.C. to 300 A.D., and the bow as well as the atlatl was apparently in use toward the end of that period, though the majority of the projectile points still weighed over 5 grams. [Hester and Heizer (14) postulate that the bow and arrow were not introduced into California until about 500-1000 A.D. Elsasser (7) suggests an earlier time, feeling that the bow and arrow, now calling for lighter tipped arrows, probably were introduced around 1500 or 2000 years ago.] The early phase of the Middle Horizon, Central California, has been considered by some to equate with the Martis Complex of the Sierra Nevada [7], since both have similar basalt projectile point types.

The "Late Horizon" is dated from 300 A.D. and on to the appearance of the White man. The artifacts now included many small obsidian arrowheads [often with deeply serrated edges] intended for the bow and arrow rather than the spear-thrower or atlatl.

Finally, the "King's Beach Complex" is named from a site at King's Beach along the north side of Lake Tahoe, and apparently represented a civilization oriented towards fishing and gathering. It existed in approximately the same time period as the Late Central California Culture further west, perhaps around 1000 A.D. or later. During this period, the projectile points suggest that the bow and arrow were by then in extensive use. This includes small, triangular notched points, often with serrated or toothed edges, and finely chipped. They also may be either leaf-shaped or stemmed points.

What is known about the projectile points that are found along the North Fork of the American River? A number of people summering in this valley, both at the Chickering camp and at the Cedars, have extensive collections of projectile points which they or their families have found over the years around the general area where the North Fork petroglyphs occur. Some seven different types of these points appear identifiable as being distinct one from the other.

The base end of the point was the means of categorizing the different styles of forming the projectile point. I have classified the points into a scheme [see Fig. p. 17] as follows: Type A is leaf-like, with no separate stem or notching. Type C is a triangular point with a concave or notched base. Type E is also

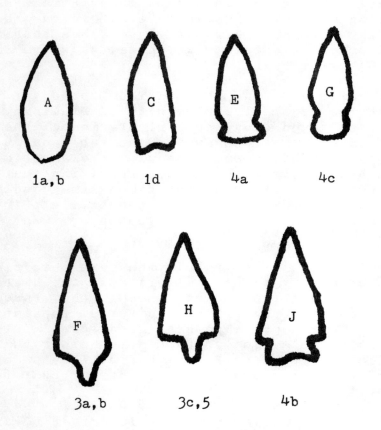

Scheme used for classifying projectile points found near the Cedars on the basis of the type of base end (with notation of the Elsasser, 15, classification of the types shown).

roughly triangular, but has side notches and a flat base. Type G may be hard to really separate from Type E--it has a rounded, convex base rather than being flat. Type F has no obvious notch, but has a contracting or nearly parallel stem, usually rounded at the end. Type H may be easily confused with Type F, since it differs primarily by having an abrupt indentation to the stem, and on occasion may have clear-cut "ears" in the notched area going back to the stem of the point. Type J has both side notches and a notched or concave base, which may show up "ears" at the base of the projectile point.

I have examined and classified three of the major collections at the Cedars. The results of examining these 234 projectile points found along the tributaries of the North Fork of the American River are shown in the table on p. 19. These represent the points that seemed useful for classification [stem end plus enough of the side, but not requiring that the tip be present] in the collections of Roberta Eastman and her mother, Mrs. Searls [and including 24 of the projectile points from that collection displayed at the Cedars clubhouse]; Ray Wilbur III; and Winslow Hall.

The results in the tabulation are exciting in the demonstration of a very close similarity in the distribution of the different projectile points among the three separate collections. Clearly, there is a diverse population of the different types of projectile points; and equally clearly, each of the collections has a similar population distribution. Type F predominates, and Type H occurs with about the same frequency. The two types of stemmed projectile points account for more than half of the total.

Another characteristic or two is important regarding these projectile points. Nearly all of them are made of basalt, with only a few of flint or chert. Only a small few were made from obsidian or red jasper. The only really tiny ones, which look like arrowheads for birds, are of obsidian [Wilbur collection]. A very large number of the projectile points are of appreciable size and heavy. More than a third of the Type F stemmed points in the Eastman and Wilbur collections were more than 5 centimeters long, and one-half of the Type A leaf-shaped projectile points were over 5 centimeters long. They do not appropriately seem to be called arrowheads. It is more likely that they were used on darts or small spears or javelins, perhaps thrown with the Indian "atlatl". This spear-throwing devise requires a heavy weight if the projectile is to be thrown to any great distance and with a fair accuracy. Only when the bow and arrow were introduced at a later period could the size of the stone projectile point be markedly reduced.

How do the Cedars projectile points relate to other prehistoric artifacts? It would appear that the period from 6000

Type Classification of Projectile Points
in Three Major Collections at
The Cedars

Type	Eastman/Searls	Wilbur	Hall	Total
	74 points	51 points	109 points	234 points
	percentage	of the points	of each type	
F	28	18	35	29
H	24	27	22	24
E	15	20	12	15
J	9	12	12	11
A	11	12	9	10
G	8	8	7	8
C	4	4	3	3

B.C. and earlier can be eliminated. There are no Folsom points, Clovis points, or Sandia points in the Cedars collections. There are no Eden points, Plainview points, or Yuma points. The peoples making these flaked points lived over much of the Southwestern states, but were not game hunters in the Sierra around the North Fork of the American River.

The Archaic Stage, covering the period 1000-7000 years ago, presents a quite different picture. A great many of the Cedars points closely resemble the points of the Martis Complex or the Early and Middle Central California Cultures. They tend to be large, many are leaf-shaped or stemmed, most are basalt and few are from obsidian, and they appear to be intended for the spear or dart. The Early California points are 4 centimeters long or larger; in the collections at the Cedars all but one of the Type A leaf-shaped points exceed this, and nearly two-thirds of the Type F shouldered or contracting stemmed points. These are the two shapes of projectile points that are typical of this period and these cultures.

Martin and co-workers [16] say that it is likely that the large projectile points of the Early California period were used on spears or spear-thrower darts, whereas the introduction of the much-smaller triangular points during the Middle period marked the first appearance of the bow and arrow in Central California. This Middle California period has included many obsidian as well as basalt or slate points; they were leaf-shaped or stemmed, and finely chipped. The Late period, perhaps beginning about 1000 A.D., includes small triangular notched points of obsidian, and often with serrated edges. Interestingly, the Wilbur collection at the Cedars includes 2 serrated or saw-toothed points, and includes 4 small, triangular obsidian points. These, and some of the other points in the Cedars and Chickerings collections, appear to relate to the latest period of occupation by ancestors of the Indians in the area during historical times.

An artifact collection by Peter Fish, nearly all collected near the Chickerings camp, greatly extends this. Again, the great majority of points are basalt and large, Martis types. However, the small points in this collection include 9 obsidian, 17 jasper, 4 basalt, and 10 chert arrowheads. Most of these are less than 5 mm. in length and are "desert side-notched" in type [a type associated with the King's Beach Complex]. The Summit Soda Springs area at the Chickerings thus appears to have had two major Indian occupations some thousands of years apart. This is not too surprising; Elston has noted that winter camps northwest of Reno [25] and along the Truckee River north of Lake Tahoe [23] clearly were occupied by both Martis and King's Beach Indians, though the King's Beach peoples probably date well after 1000 A.D., far later than the Martis Indians.

The most provocative, and perhaps also productive, lead to

connect the North Fork projectile points with a known and dated prehistoric period is the marked resemblance to the Martis Complex. Heizer and Elsasser [17] listed data on more than 800 projectile points found at the original Martis site near Truckee [designated Pla-5], and published a photograph of the types of points. This photo is strikingly similar to pictures I have taken of the limited collections of the Pinehurst family, of the Fishes at Chickerings, and the Eastman-Searls [see p. 22] and the Wilbur collections from the Cedars. They clearly appear to be from a common culture. Indeed, there are many threads of similarity to suggest that the Martis-site people and those who hunted along the North Fork of the American River were related. Both sites, incidentally, are in Placer County of California and only some 20 miles apart [but separated by the Sierra crest].

When I compared the projectile point types of those near the Cedars with the classification and findings of Heizer and Elsasser at the original Martis site, as well as another major Martis site excavated in the California foothills, the table on p. 23 clearly suggests the marked similarity. For each set, nearly all of the leaf-shaped points were with a rounded base [Heizer-Elsasser Type 1b]. For each, nearly all shouldered points were with rounded or squared ends [Types 3a and 3b]. The major barbed points had the stem projecting beyond the level of the barbs [Type 5a], for each set. And each set was predominantly of heavy points much more likely to be for use with the atlatl spear-thrower than for a bow. The sets are nearly all of basalt, and with only a tiny few obsidian or jasper points.

The evidence strongly suggests that the North Fork points represent another "site area" for the Martis Complex. [Hester and Heizer (14) remind us that the Martis series is very much in need of further detailed study.]

Incidentally, a great many Martis Complex sites now have been identified. Heizer and Elsasser [17] in 1953 listed 6 in Nevada County and 6 in Placer County. Elsasser [15] in 1960 mapped several dozen "Martis-affiliated" sites, a half-dozen of which had been excavated [Fig. p. 24].

The Martis Complex is typified by use of basalt as preferred material for chipped implements; rare use of obsidian or chert; fairly large and heavy projectile points, and roughly chipped; expanded-base finger-held flaked drills or punches. Though one boatstone or atlatl weight was found at the original Martis site, Elsasser [15] notes that several excavations in the Martis area over a period of several years failed to yield any boatstones. He had expected that such a weight would be associated with the heavy Martis-type points, suggestive of atlatl darts and a weighted throwing stick. The spear-thrower is effective without an added weight, however. No boatstone-type weight is in the collections from the North Fork watershed. Incidentally, a basalt

21

Some of the Basalt Projectile Points
Found at the Cedars

A Comparison of the Relative Distribution of Projectile Points at Martis Sites and Those at the North Fork Sites

Point type	Martis type-site, Pla-5 [17]	Foothills site, Nev-15 [15]	North Fork sites*
Leaf-shaped	20%	3%	15%
Triangular	2	5	3
Shouldered	34	35	47
Side-notched	37	18	25
Barbed or tanged	5	39	10
Average length in mm.			
Leaf-shaped	58 mm.	43 mm.	52 mm.
Shouldered	50	37	47
Side-notched	45	39	44
Average width in mm.			
Leaf-shaped	20 mm.	17 mm.	19 mm.
Shouldered	20	19	21
Side-notched	21	22	22
	849 points	213 points	200 points

* From the Eastman/Searls, Pinehurst, Fish, Hall, Gortner collections.

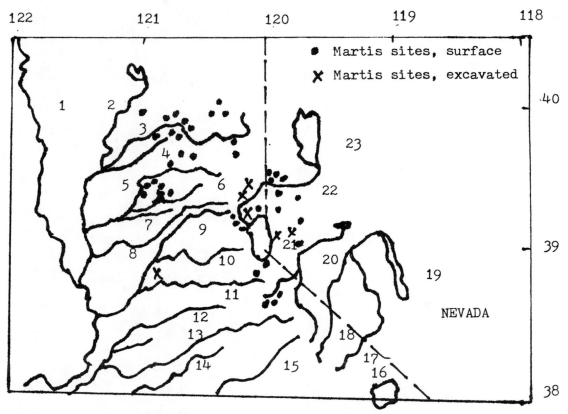

Distribution of Martis Complex Sites Known in 1960
(Adapted from Elsasser, 15)

Key to rivers and lakes	
1 Sacramento River	12 Consumnes River
2 North Fork, Feather River	13 Mokelumne River
3 Middle Fork, Feather River	14 Calaveras River
4 South Fork, Feather River	15 Stanislaus River
5 North Fork, Yuba River	16 Mono Lake
6 Middle Fork, Yuba River	17 East Walker River
7 South Fork, Yuba River	18 West Walker River
8 Bear River	19 Walker Lake
9 North Fork, American River	20 Carson River
10 Middle Fork, American River	21 Lake Tahoe
11 South Fork, American River	22 Truckee River
	23 Pyramid Lake

drill or awl in 3 of the collections appear identical with those found at the Martis site [17, Plate 1B].

The tapered stemmed points so common along the North Fork are considered [11] as a form quite typical of the Martis Complex, although it may occur all over the North Sierra and include the California foothill areas. It accounted for 27 percent of the points at the Auburn site Pla-101, and was designated by Ritter and Matson [11] as the "Martis Contracting Stemmed Point Form" diagnostic of the Martis Complex.

What do these artifacts tell us about the age of the petroglyphs along the North Fork? The many projectile points found in this area where there are extensive petroglyph carvings suggest that both were made by the early ancestors of the present-day Indians. Archaeological evidence, supported by radiochemical dating at other sites having comparable artifact evidence [7, 8, 11, 23, 26] suggests that this part of the Sierra was hunted extensively during the summer months perhaps 3500 years ago.

It is with awe that we realize that some of the North Fork petroglyphs were carved at about the same time that the pharoah, Tutankhamen, reigned in Egypt; a thousand years before Alexander the Great's conquest of Asia Minor; thirty centuries before Columbus discovered America.

A minor part of the projectile point collections clearly points to a more recent but limited occupancy of the region, 1000 A.D. and on up to the time when the White man came to California.

Obviously, the Indians from the Late Central California Culture or the King's Beach Complex could have made the petro-glyphs along the North Fork of the American River [though only a limited number of projectile points indicate their presence along the North Fork]. Nevertheless, the area was inhabited and hunted much more extensively by Indians of the Martis Complex, or the Early and Middle Central California Cultures, and it is not unreasonable to expect that most if not all of the petroglyphs go back to that time. Indeed, the ethnohistory of the later tribal groups indicates they did not make petroglyphs.

Thus the North Fork Indian artifacts, ie., projectile points, clearly suggest that the petroglyphs date back to the period 2000 B.C. to 1000 B.C. This receives support from a dating of the styles of symbols in the petroglyphs [p. 13], since the styles also suggest that the petroglyph could be 2000 years or more old [1000 B.C. to 1500 A.D. proposed for the Great Basin Curvilinear Abstract style].

In the book edited by Clewlow [5], Heizer and Hester say that the carving of petroglyphs was given up in late prehistoric times; this is why the dating of California and Nevada petroglyphs stops around 1500 A.D. These authors try to speculate why the pecking of petroglyphs discontinued throughout the Great Basin area. They suggest that the practice may have been abandoned because a change in hunting methods or areas may have made the petroglyphs "unnecessary" by the tribal traditions or rituals. I wonder whether the introduction of the bow and arrow might not be such a drastic change, for it permitted greater accuracy in killing game, and from a much greater distance than use of the atlatl spear-throwing technique required previously. The average distance of flight for the atlatl-spear is about 70-80 yards, and the accuracy will be good only for much shorter distances, perhaps 20-30 yards. The arrow from a bow may easily have a flight more than twice as much and with greater accuracy, and hence killing power.

As the spear-thrower atlatl became obsolete, perhaps around 500 A.D., the introduction of the bow and arrow would have been responsible for a major change in hunting habits and food supply of the prehistoric Indians who previously had spent their summers hunting along the American River. We know that such a major change did take place, for only a few of the small arrowheads associated with the period of 1000 A.D. to historic times have been found along the North Fork, although hundreds of projectile points of a much earlier time were found there.

Deer would be much easier to kill with the bow and arrow, and might thus be more easily taken in the foothills nearer to the more permanent, winter homes of the Indians. The killing of small game, such as rabbits and birds, would also be possible with the improved weapons, and these could be obtained in greater quantity near the foothills than in the mountainous parts of the Sierra. At any rate, the prehistoric Indian for the most part deserted the area around the North Fork of the American River well before 1000 A.D. It is of interest that Elsasser reported [15] that

Around A.D. 800 the Martis Complex elements in the Oro-ville region seem to have been almost entirely supplan-ted.

Elston [8] considered the Early Martis Complex as beginning about 1000 B.C. and lasting until A.D. 1; later [23] this was revised to about 2000 B.C. by other radiocarbon dates.

If the petroglyphs are thousands of years old, why do some now appear to be rapidly disappearing? Long-time members of the Cedars community along the North Fork of the American River claim that the readily accessible petroglyphs, notably by the river [Site #7, p. 30] at a favorite spot of the Cedars families for swimming, are becoming less and less visible and the granite

26

crust on which they had been incised is rapidly exfoliating, with the crust breaking away. If this can happen within one person's lifetime, it is reasonable to wonder whether the rock carvings can indeed be truly ancient.

An important consideration here is that there is no way of knowing the original state of these petroglyphs when the Indians carved them in the granite. All are fully exposed to weathering. There is no way to know how deep the carvings went, and no way to even know the nature or original hardness of the granite rock itself.

Granite is an igneous rock and is composed of a mixture of quartz and mica, but more importantly contains appreciable amounts of alkaline and sodium-rich feldspars. These occur in crystalline masses in granite, and the mineral masses break rather easily. In the chemical and physical weathering of granite, it forms an onion-like layering because of the leaching away of the more-soluble alkaline salts of the feldspar; a stained and often rust-colored exterior is formed. This is the condition of much of the granite rocks along the North Fork where petroglyphs are found. Following the last ice age, it would take many centuries for weathering to alter the smoothly polished granite and develop the crusts and the alkali-depleted layer. [One wonders whether the "acid rains" that have been associated with recent urban civilization may have markedly accelerated the leaching and weathering process.]

Once the crust-like layer is formed, any cracks will allow surface water and melting snow to more easily get into the rock and under the crust. With freezing, the 10 percent expansion of water when it becomes ice can then start the process of breaking the crust away from the major underlying granite. This is a self-perpetuating mechanism, for with the first cracking of the crust, greater access of water and ice to the remaining underlying parts of the crust is to be expected. Thus, the early weathering and breakage can be an extremely slow process, but the last aspects of it can go quite rapidly.

While most of the petroglyphs along the North Fork are on granite rocks, some of the rock carvings occur on basalt. This is a dark grey or greenish-black rock; it frequently may have filled a large cavity in the granite when it was formed. It does not have the large concentration of alkaline feldspar, and consequently does not leach and weather to form the crusting seen on granite. In the several sites along the North Fork of the American River where petroglyphs were carved in the basalt rather than the granite portion of the rock, the petroglyph even today is quite clear and often appreciably deeper than the symbols carved on granite. Perhaps the basalt petroglyphs are better indications of the great age of the rock carvings.

Of course, another very significant feature needs to be recognized in the rapid decline for some of the petroglyphs, such as at Site #7. This is the considerable traffic over the site for many years, with many people walking over the petroglyphs, and frequently wearing hiking boots. A few decades of this human insensitivity to an archaeological, prehistoric evidence of early man in California may explain in itself the gradual disappearance of many of the carvings. The major petroglyph panel designated Site #27 [p. 30] further upstream on the river has far less erosion and the carvings remain relatively clear, even though the site was well known and described in the mid-1880's. That petroglyph site has relatively little human traffic, in marked contrast to the petroglyphs at Site #7.

VI. WHERE ARE THE PETROGLYPHS FOUND?

My field study has covered a relatively small part of Placer County, California--the lands around the headwaters of the North Fork of the American River and its tributaries. From its origin at Mountain Meadow Lake near the Sierra crest overlooking Lake Tahoe on the east, the river descends westerly about 10 miles to the area termed the Royal Gorge.

Nearly all of the land through which the river flows is privately held and posted; this is also true for most of the streams and creeks feeding the North Fork. The major landholder is the Cedars community [the North Fork Association]. Immediately adjoining this on the east are lands held by the Foulks family [Pinehurst Association], and adjoining them upstream all the way up to and including Mountain Meadow Lake , far up the mountain and near the Sierra crest, is the land of the Chickering family. The summer homes of the Chickerings occupy the site of the old Mark Hopkins-Summit Soda Springs Hotel, popular in the late 1880's. A few of the lands adjoining some of the tributaries belong to the U.S. Forest Service. This, then, is where some 46 sites for the North Fork Indian petroglyphs have been found [see Fig. p. 30].

There are two reasons why such an intensive study was made for such a small area. One of these was referred to in the introductory section, namely that only by such evidence from a detailed study of a smaller region than a whole state can further understanding derive of the significance and history of petroglyph carvings in the West.

More importantly, however, was the personal fun, interest, and satisfaction that I had in researching and searching the North Fork petroglyphs, with countless hikes through the woods and mountains of this wilderness area along the North Fork of the American River to discover and rediscover petroglyph sites and to record [sometimes painfully, but always time consuming] each of the symbols or carvings on the rocks. And the study has involved the enjoyment of many hours in many libraries searching out knowledge of the many interrelationships of the geology, the Indian legends, their totems, their culture, and their various projectile points and other artifacts with the hope that they might give a clue to some of the many questions which will occur to an observer of this Indian rock art form.

In all of the writings from Heizer's associates at the University of California-Berkeley, the conclusion is made that the petroglyphs are along game trails and associated with a ceremonial or magical motivation for the taking of game. Heizer and Baumhoff [2] say,

We admit that every single occurrence of petroglyphs in

29

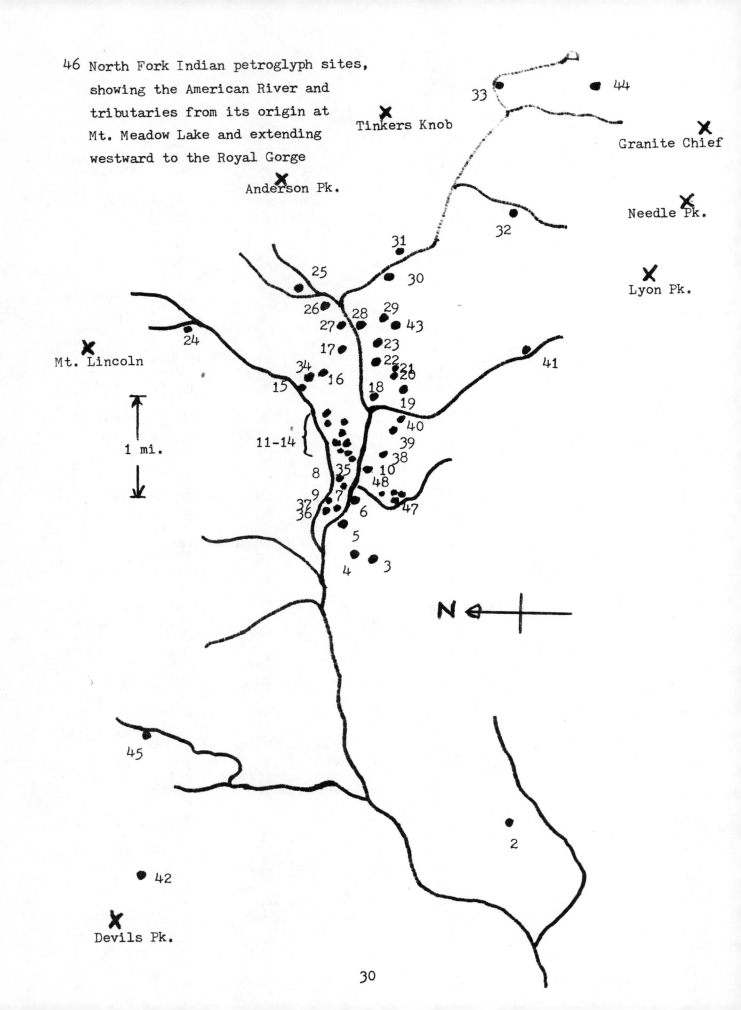

46 North Fork Indian petroglyph sites, showing the American River and tributaries from its origin at Mt. Meadow Lake and extending westward to the Royal Gorge

Nevada cannot be directly and conclusively proved to be associated with the taking of game animals, but at the same time we think the evidence...overwhelmingly supports this conclusion.

Heizer and Hester [5] reiterate this, hypothesizing that in this area most of the petroglyph sites exist where seasonally migrating deer moving between summer and winter ranges could be killed. I might add that the area bordering the North Fork of the American River abounds with deer in the summer, and thus any of the petroglyphs found there will be close to a logical game trail.

One of the conclusions proposed by Heizer and Baumhoff [2] fails to jibe with petroglyph findings along the North Fork. They failed to find any petroglyphs along the eastern slopes of the Sierra Nevada near Lake Tahoe and on south towards Yosemite. They rationalize this by saying that in such summer camps [5000 to 8000 feet in elevation] the deer could be hunted singly and without a communal hunt; thus the petroglyph magic would have been ineffective. Such an area would be true for the North Fork headwaters, and yet I have found many dozens of petroglyph sites along hunting trails there.

Were the North Fork petroglyph sites known previously? Other than the extensive rock carvings at the Donner Summit [Site #1], only one of the sites was really well known--that at the Chickerings [#27]. One other major site [#22] was studied in a limited way many years ago by a graduate student archaeologist in California, but his thesis [24] was not publicized or written up in scientific journals.

Mallery [1] in his 1888 report on Indian picture-writing quotes a description of the Chickering petroglyphs [designated Pla-26 by Steward (18), and as Site #27 in my listing of North Fork petroglyph sites] and others in the region:

> The best known and largest collection of marks that I know of covers a large smooth ledge at Hopkins Soda Springs, 12 miles south of the summit on the Central Pacific railroad. The rock is much the same in character as those I have described, but the groundwork in this case is a solid ledge 10 feet one way and perhaps 40 the other, all closely covered with rude characters, many of which seem to point to human figures, animals, reptiles, etc. The ledge lies at an angle of 45°, and must have been a tempting place for a lazy artist who chanced that way.

> Many other places on the Truckee river have such rocks all very much alike, and yet each bearing its own distinct features in the marking. Near a rock half a

mile east of Verdi, a station on the Central Pacific
railroad, 10 miles east (sic!) of Reno, lie two others,
the larger of which has lines originating in a hole at
the upper right-hand corner, all running in tangents and
angles, making a double-ended kind of an arrangement of
many-headed arrows, pointing three ways. A snail-like
scroll lies between the two arms, but does not touch
them. Below are blotches, as if the artist had tried his
tools.

This region has been roamed over by the Washoe
Indians from a remote period, but none of them know
anything of these works. One who has gray hair and more
wrinkles than hairs, who is bent with age and who is
said to be a hundred years old, was led to the spot. He
said he saw them a heap long time ago, when he was only
a few summers old, and they looked then just as they do
now.

<u>Where should one look to find such petroglyphs?</u> In making
this study, almost every significant rocky outcropping [and
indeed, each major boulder] was deemed worthy of attention. As
the number of sites identified became greater, it was evident
that greatest success in locating a petroglyph site came when a
few suitable conditions were met.

The area had to have a clear view of one or more of the
major peaks surrounding the headwaters of the North Fork. With no
exception, each of the sites that were discovered was within 20-
30 feet of a magnificent view of an important mountain, and
frequently a panorama of the peaks--Mount Lincoln, Crow's Nest,
Anderson Peak, Tinkers Knob, Granite Chief, Needles Peak, Lyon
Peak, Snow Mountain, and Devils Peak. Any outdoor person at such
a spot will be thrilled by such a sight; the prehistoric Indians
who left these petroglyphs must have had some of the same
feelings of awe, or it was incorporated in their religion.
Apparently the Indians did not use the major peaks themselves, or
the heights of the ridge, as petroglyph sites. The view of the
peak was important, but being on the peak itself was not. Being
near a hunting trail was much more important.

A second criterion is the presence of an open rock
outcropping. None of the petroglyphs occurs on even a huge rock
boulder that would seem to be suitable. They only occur on
bedrock. None will be found on a cliff or a vertical part of an
outcroppping. They only occur on either flat, horizontal rock or
a gently sloping rock.

While the great majority of the petroglyphs are on granite
that has weathered to give it a pinkish surface, the rock
carvings also may be in the dark grey basaltic rock, so this
should not be overlooked. Indeed, some five dozen of the

individual petroglyph symbols [glyphs] along the North Fork of the American River encompass a basalt area within the granite, frequently in a very innovative way [Fig. p. 34]. The dark circular basalt spot may have rays suggesting the sun, or rain from a cloud; may constitute the palm of a bear paw; may be the head of a sperm-like symbol; may form the head of a centipede-like symbol; and two basalt spots may be connected with an undulating carved line.

Do these criteria for a petroglyph site differ from other areas where petroglyphs are found? Yes. I have never seen any reference in other accounts of Indian petroglyphs which makes any mention of a view or panorama which might have had an influence on the choice of a particular rocky area. Many of the site descriptions, especially within the books by Heizer and his co-workers, make it evident that no inspirational view was at all likely.

The North Fork petroglyphs may also be distinguished from other petroglyph sites because they only appear on bedrock. Elsewhere, boulders [and often small boulders] have been used. This may be seen in illustrations in the book by Mallery [1, pages 59 and 61 illustrate petroglyphs in California, and on pages 76, 108, and 109 one can see rock carvings on boulders at other places], as well as the book by Heizer and Baumhoff [2], particularly seen in the photographs in their Plates 1-3, 5, 8-13, 20-24. Their photographs also show the rock carvings on nearly vertical faces, and some on cliff sides [Plates 2, 5, 12-14, 17-21]. Here again, maybe the North Fork petroglyphs are some what unique, since they are never found on boulders or vertical rock faces or cliffs.

Are the petroglyphs near identifiable Indian campsites? Here the answer is both yes and no. The two largest petroglyph areas along the North Fork, with hundreds of individual symbols or carvings, are near Log Cabin Creek [Site #6], and at Site #27, by the river and near where the Chickering family summer cabins are. Both of these are near major campsites of the early Indians, evidenced by the hundreds of projectile points that have been found in the neighborhood of these two petroglyph sites. Yet extensive rock carvings are found on two major rock outcroppings overlooking the river on Pinehurst property [Sites #22 and #23], and these do not seem to be near an Indian camp, and projectile points or other flaked artifacts have not been found here.

Heizer and Baumhoff [2] state that the petroglyphs do not commonly occur where people camped; the Nevada petroglyphs usually are at spots with no evidence of occupation, probably for the very good reason that most of those sites are unfavorable for such camping. This may be true for the desert, but it is not true for the woods and streams of the North Fork watershed in the Sierra.

Some Examples of the Use of Basalt Inclusions
in Petroglyph Symbols

A great many of the petroglyph sites along the North Fork of the American River involve only a very few carvings or symbols on a rock outcropping, sometimes only a single glyph; these sites seem even less likely to be associated with any major campground of the prehistoric Indians hunting in this area.

Wherever major Indian camps have been identified, nearby outcroppings should be looked at for possible petroglyphs; sites that are otherwise suitable but not associated with an early Indian camp should never be ignored, however.

Are the petroglyph sites also game ambush sites? Several lines of reasoning have led me to consider this possibility. Other than actually running down the game, the limitations of using only a spear or dart thrower to kill the game meant that the hunter had to be in fairly open ground to throw the spear, had to be perhaps as close to the game as 20 yards, yet had to avoid scaring the game away before making the attempt at a kill. I remembered that the petroglyph sites were in open, unwooded areas, were on elevated outcroppings, and many had a rather precipitous face with brush or trails some 10 feet below the granite rock. On three occasions when I was examining petroglyphs I startled a buck deer just below me, and within easy distance for a possible kill had I been a hunter armed with a spear thrower. The hunter might not even need to be camouflaged, since he could kneel on the rock, facing the wind, and wait until a deer passed underneath the sheer face of the outcropping.

In view of this possibility, I revisited the petroglyph sites, specifically examining whether each might be suitable for hunting game with primitive weapons. For many of the sites [but certainly not all], ambush of game clearly was suitable from the petroglyph outcroppings themselves. Many sites had clearly marked deer trails within yards of the elevated rock outcroppings, and below the sheer face. Yet no projectile point was found within throwing range of these petroglyphs. True, brush and pine needles now covered much of the ground and would hide any artifacts there. But the lack of evidence of actual hunting from the petroglyph rock itself leaves the ambush possibility in limbo.

Are basalt quarries near the petroglyphs? In two instances, basalt sources for the prehistoric Indian flaked tools and points were found near petroglyph sites [#32 and #41]. Large boulders of basalt had been broken into rocks about the size of one's head, and numerous basalt cores had been taken from them. The Indian toolmaker obviously used these cores at some other site--e.g., near Site #35 were copious basalt flakes and artifacts from such a workshop.

VII. WHAT TYPES OF SYMBOLS ARE FOUND IN THE CARVINGS?

Scale drawings of each symbol and at each petroglyph site are presented in Appendix B of this book. Some 1700 glyphs at 48 locations are included.

Not surprisingly, few of the symbols in the petroglyph panels are nearly identical. Yet there have been serious attempts by many archaeologists to categorize the symbols and their styles in the hopes of finding something of significance in their meaning or chronology.

Classification of the symbols into "elements". Heizer and Baumhoff [2] state that

Definition of styles requires a preliminary step: analysis of the corpus of materials into design elements... Our typology is basically a modification of that proposed by Steward [1929] for the petroglyphs of the western United States. We have added some new elements and have modified or subdivided others until we feel the classification is suitable for known Nevada petroglyphs.

I have used this 1962 classification system of Heizer and Baumhoff [see Table p. 37] for the thousand or more individual symbols or carvings on petroglyphs along the North Fork of the American River. This has been fruitful in ascribing the petroglyphs into "styles", and thus to assist in projecting an age range for the rock carvings [p. 13]. However, I strongly concur with the observation of Heizer and Clewlow [3] that a great many of the symbols will not receive the same classification by two independent investigators, or even by the same investigator at two times. And a great many of the symbols are not as simple as the "design element" list, but rather are combinations, or even unlisted elements [e.g., parallel wavy or curving lines].

Three of the symbols that are found in large numbers on North Fork petroglyphs are the sun disc [element 12], the rake [33], and the paw [47]. The problem in classifying these supposedly straightforward glyphs is illustrated in the drawings [pp.38-40], which represent tracings of the 1:10 scale drawings of the symbols of various petroglyphs along the North Fork.

The definition of a rake clearly would fit both A and B [Fig. p. 38]. In C the horizontal line is markedly convex, and in D is markedly concave. In E, G, and M the vertical lines are much longer than the horizontal line. In F and L the horizontal line is greatly extended, and L now has the vertical lines as parallel wavy lines. In H the curving vertical lines are not parallel, but in J the beautiful wavy lines parallel each other. K also has parallel curving lines, but now has another horizontal line that

Design Elements Used in
Petroglyph Classification by Heizer and Baumhoff [2]

---

1. Circle
2. Concentric circles
3. Bisected circle
4. Sectioned circle
5. Spoked circle
6. Spoked concentric circles
7. Tailed circle
8. Circle and dot
9. Circle cluster *
10. Connected circles
11. Chain of circles
12. Sun disc
13. Spiral
14. Curvilinear meander
15. Convoluted rake
16. Connected dots *
17. Dumbbell *
18. Dots or dot design *
19. Wavy lines
20. Deer hoof
21. Oval grid
22. Rectangular grid
23. Blocked oval *
24. Cross
25. Bird tracks
26. Parallel straight lines
27. Triangles
28. Lozenge chain
29. Zigzag lines
30. Star or asterisk
31. Ladder, one pole
32. Ladder, two poles
33. Rake
34. Rain symbol
35. Rectilinear meander
36. Chevrons
37. Radiating dashes
38. Crosshatching
39. Plant form
40. Bird *
41. Lizard
42. Mountain sheep
43. Sheep horns *
44. Quadruped [not sheep] *
45. Snake
46. Many-legged insect
47. Foot or paw
48. Hand *
49. Human *
50. Horned human *
51. Human stick figure
52. Human, stick limbs *
53. Katchina figure *
54. White man *
55. Atlatl *
56. Arrow *
57. Deer *
58. Fish *

---

* These design elements as defined in [2] are not seen in the North Fork petroglyphs.

Which of These is Properly Categorized as a RAKE? "A horizontal line with shorter lines extending vertically down from it...The crossbar is occasionally diagonal rather than horizontal" (2).

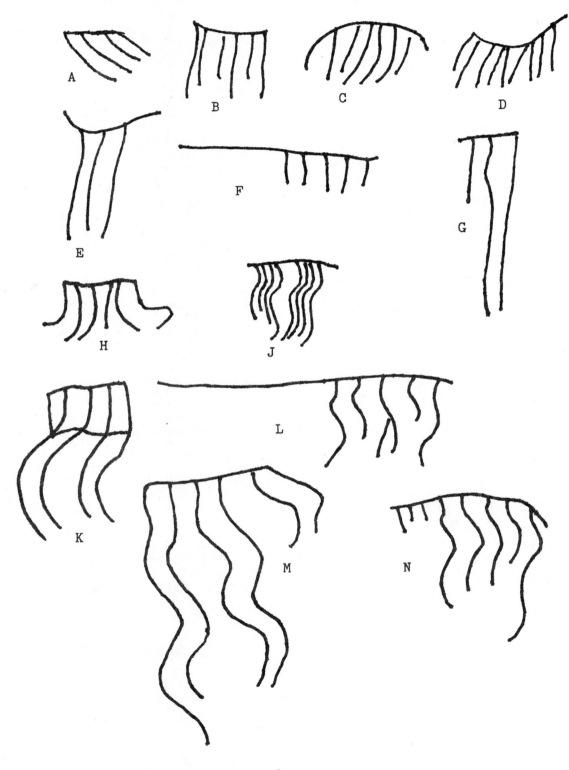

Which of These is Properly Categorized as a SUN DISC? "A circle with several lines radiating from its perimeter" (2).

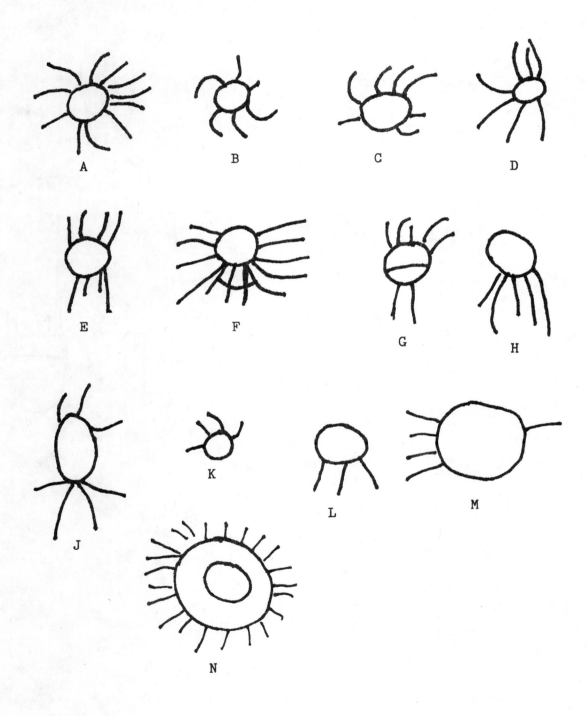

Which of These is Properly Categorized as a PAW? "Usually resembles a bear paw, with a large palm and short toes or claws" (2).

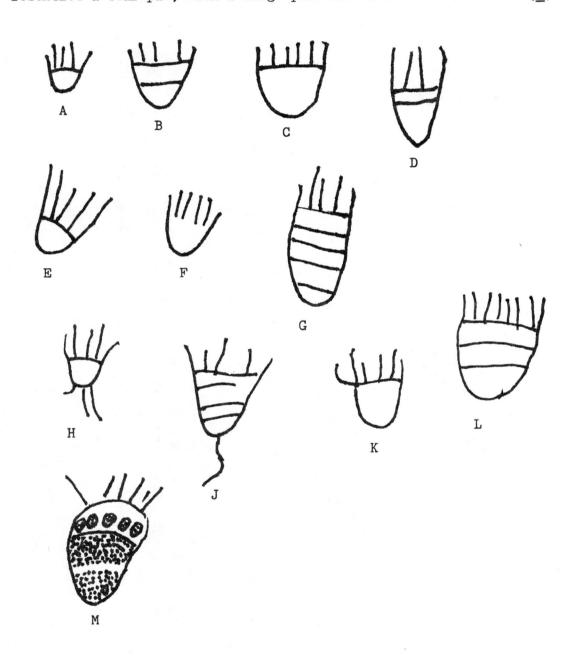

forms a box near the top. M has parallel curving lines but also other parallel curving lines that mirror the first set. And N has some short vertical lines and a number of longer wavy lines as well.

The sun disc also poses problems of classification [Fig. p. 39]. A is a classical concept of a sun, yet is not frequently seen. B has rays curving strongly. C, ,D and E have rays for only part of the circle. In F we see a line connecting several of the "rays", and in G a line bisects the disc. H, J, K, and L have few lines and not extending around the circle; M is similar but also has a "ray" opposite to the others. The sun disc in N differs from the others in having two concentric circles as the "sun". One wonders whether all of these examples are intended to depict the same thing to the makers of the petroglyphs. Yet they may well be classified as a single design element--the sun disc.

The paw poses a classification problem too [Fig. p. 40]. A is as expected. B differs in having the palm divided into two parts. Nature would limit the number of claws to 5, but the early Indian seemed not to be so constrained, as witness C and K and L, with more than 5, and D with only 4 "claws". [It might be noted that Grant (20) shows "bear track" petroglyph symbols with both 4 and 5 claws. He says that often one finds that the paw pad is divided by a lateral center line, and that the toe pads may be replaced by curving claws such as are associated with a grizzly bear track.] In E the claw is greatly elongated; in F it has no clear marking of the palm. The palm normally would have at most one subdivision, but the paw symbols in some glyphs may have many lines across the palm, such as in G, J, and L. Is it still a "bear paw" when there is a tail extending from the palm, such as in H and J? Are the curving lines in K still representing claws? Again, one wonders whether these diversities might not indicate that quite different meanings were intended [by the early Indian] for many of the symbols stylistically typed [by the archaeologist] into single "design elements".

And surprisingly, only a single symbol [M] seems to fairly faithfully depict a grizzly bear track. A photograph in the August 1981 issue of Smithsonian Magazine shows a grizzly bear footprint, with five toe pads, lines below these and further down on the palm pad, and five claw markings above the toe pads--and the photo markedly resembles this one glyph at Site #27.

In hopes of eliminating some of the classification uncertainties, I tried to merge some of the 58 design elements, such as combining #3-6. The condensed categories that resulted had some usefulness, but the problem of uncertain classification for many symbols still remained. Details of the attempted revision are not worth being presented here.

Nevertheless, classification schemes can be condensed too

much. I was surprised and somewhat disappointed to find that in 1978 Heizer and Clewlow [3] had discarded the detailed "58 element" scheme and decided to classify the California petroglyphs only into 5 element categories--human, animal, circle-and-dot, angular, and curvilinear. Four revised petroglyph "styles" were now proposed for California rock art--Great Basin, Central Sierran, Southwest Coast, North Coast.

Distribution of the symbols at different sites. The Heizer-Baumhoff element classification was used to analyze the symbols on the North Fork petroglyphs. Only selected findings from the resulting table of design elements vs. site will be mentioned.

On reflection it is easy to see that the statistical approach of examining the relative distribution of the North Fork petroglyph symbols would place overwhelming emphasis on just a tiny few of the sites. The two extensive petroglyph panels at Sites #6 and #27 account for more than half of the symbols observed on petroglyph rocks in the watershed of the North Fork [which means not including the ones at Donner (#1) and near Cisco Grove (#46), along the Yuba River]. This might leave fully half of the rock carving sites as having no significance in the tabulation of use of different elements, since they have no more than 5 symbols per site. Yet those locations and those carvings may be the most important of all if someone is to research the symbols [all of which are illustrated in the Appendix] and come up with an educated guess of why they were made and, especially, what they may signify. One writer [19] said he had no success in deciphering symbols on large panels, but rather found "keys" [to him] by studying petroglyphs consisting of only one or two symbols, since these "had to be complete in themselves".

The tabulation which I made of the distribution of the design elements among symbols found at the 48 sites [46 of which are along the North Fork of the American River or its tributaries] did bring out a few differences between those sites having only a very few symbols [10 or less design elements] and the ones having an appreciable number [30 or more]. Thirteen of the design elements were not seen at all on the 28 sites with very few symbols, yet they appeared 89 times on the 12 sites having many symbols on the rock. For example, the glyphs categorized as spiral, deer hoof, chevron, and snake appeared frequently at many sites, but only when the rock carvings included many symbols, never in those sites with 10 or less glyphs. Perhaps such differences can suggest something in considering what the different symbols may mean.

Some marked difference in the use of the rock art design elements also can be seen when comparing the petroglyphs near known early Indian campsites [Sites #6, 27] with the remainder of the North Fork petroglyph sites. Twice as many sun discs and human stick figures are found at Sites #6 and #27 as in all of the other petroglyph sites. On the other hand, nearly twice as many spirals and lozenge chains are found at sites other than the two major camp areas. Sites #6 and #27 account for three-fourths of the bear paw symbols, whereas four-fifths of the symbols with parallel wavy lines and essentially all of the bird track glyphs are at sites other than these two campsite locations.

The petroglyph sites by Donner Summit [Site #1] and near Cisco Grove [#46] were included in the study of North Fork petroglyphs even though they are not on a tributary of the North Fork of the American River and not even in Placer County, as all the other locations are. Their physical locations suggest that the Donner Pass was a logical point of passage across the Sierra Nevada even for the early Indians, and the carvings there might have been the work of either the ancestors of the Washo, the desert tribe on the Nevada side of the Sierra, or the Maidu or Miwok, the tribes from the foothills on the California side of the Sierra Nevada range. It was hoped that the distribution of the petroglyph symbols at Donner and Cisco Grove versus those at major sites by the North Fork [especially those at Sites #6 and #27] might give a clue as to the people making these carvings.

The Donner petroglyphs have relatively fewer circles-with-rays, or sun discs; and fewer paws than at the two major North Fork sites; but have more use of spirals. The Donner petroglyphs have many more parallel wavy lines. In this respect, the use of symbols on the Donner petroglyphs tends to resemble the group of North Fork petroglyphs that are not associated with a major prehistoric campsite. But the general similarity of the style at the Donner and the North Fork sites attests to the two peoples probably being of a similar culture [Martis?]. A similar style is seen in the site across the Old Highway 40 from Sugar Bowl [Nev-85, Heizer and Clewlow (3), Fig. 186], along the probable passage across the Sierra.

The rock carvings on the South Fork of the Yuba River [Site #46] also bear a resemblance to the style used in the glyphs along the North Fork of the American River, such as its use of various circle elements, but is noted for its absence of any "rake" symbols. Of possible importance for interpreting the carvings [see p. 68] is the human stick figure [p. 174], the only such glyph clearly associated with two other symbols--the chevron and the two joined circles [one having two rays]. These latter symbols occur alone at several sites, but never together with the human figure.

It is also evident that two major North Fork petroglyph sites, both of which are near known early Indian campsites and each of which has hundreds of individual carvings in the granite rock outcropping, are not absolutely identical when the distribution of the various "elements" is examined. A summary table [p. 44] indicates that most categories show a very similar

Comparison of Symbols at Major Petroglyph
Sites and Near Campgrounds along the North Fork

Symbol	Site #6	Site #27
	percent of the total	
Circles [incl. concentric, tailed, connected circles]	20	19
Divided circles [incl. bisected,, sectioned, spoked circles]	12	10
Sun discs	11	9
Paws	10	12
Enclosed grids	1	3
Zigzag lines	1	2
Rakes	11	4

frequency of use. One symbol stands out as quite distinct--rakes. This symbol is used quite often at the extensive carvings at Site #6, but is much less frequent in the petroglyphs at Site #27. There is no doubt at all from this tabulation that the Indians who made the two sets of carvings were the same tribal group. They followed the same style, with the same types of symbols. If they were only doodles or graffiti, this would be far less likely. But something about Site #6 [or its visitors, or its significance in use] made it favorable for the "rake" symbol-- much more than the extensively used and major rock carvings at Site #27. Again, this might offer a tiny clue on the meaning for this one symbol.

While on the subject of rake symbols, it was observed that about a fifth of them are markedly curved and many are distinctly wavy, with the wavy lines paralleling each other. Some 16 sites had these rakes that differ from the more conventional ones, but only 3 had more than a single curved or wavy rake glyph. These three were at Sites #1, 6, and 22. [Fig. p. 46].

The difference among the presumed paw symbols has already been mentioned [p. 41]. Among the sites with what appear to be clearly bear paw symbols, only two have paws with more than 5 claws. These two are the campground sites, #6 and #27; most had 6 claws, but a tiny few had 7 or 8 claws there. About a fourth of the paw symbols at North Fork petroglyph sites had fewer than 5 claws, most frequently only 4; but weathering may well have hidden some shallow claw markings for them.

Another distinct feature of the paw symbols is the presence of one or more lines across the palm in roughly half of the symbols. One cross line is by far the most frequent, but 2 lines is common at Site #27, and even 4 or 5 is seen at least once.

<u>Do these petroglyphs conform to a particular "style"?</u> As noted earlier [p. 13], Heizer and Baumhoff discussed 3 style patterns in petroglyph carvings--Great Basin Pecked, Great Basin Scratched, and Pit-and-Groove. They further subdivided the Great Basin pecked into Great Basin Representational and Great Basin Abstract, the latter being either Curvilinear or Rectilinear. These authors felt that certain symbols could characterize these different styles, as noted in the following table [p. 47]. Their suggested ages are also shown, as Heizer and Baumhoff interpreted the archaeological data then available.

A glance at the definitive elements for these different styles of petroglyphs in the West tells us that the North Fork petroglyphs may fit any one of them except the pit-and-groove style, which is not evident at all.

Rakes with Wavy, Parallel Lines

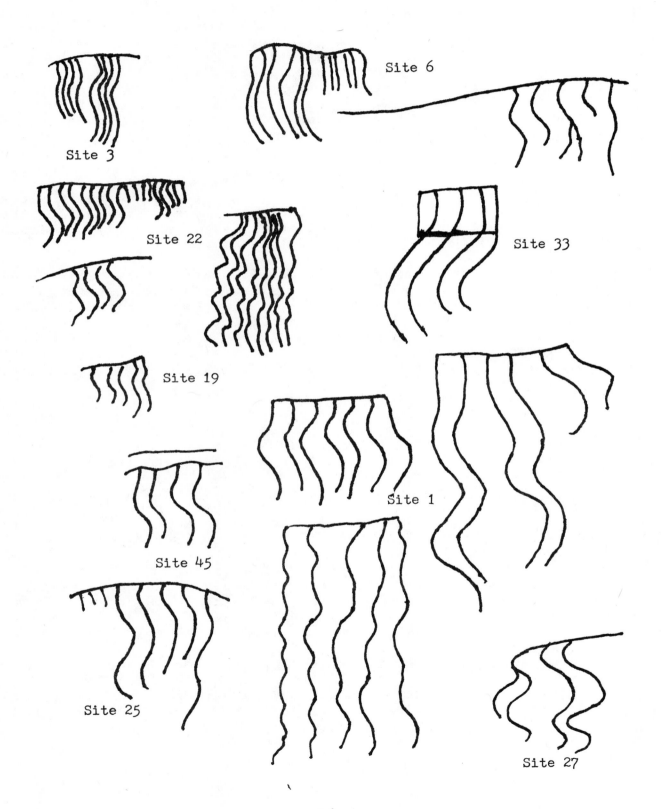

Site 3

Site 6

Site 22

Site 33

Site 19

Site 45

Site 1

Site 25

Site 27

Style Characteristics and Suggested Dating
[Heizer and Baumhoff, 2]

Style	Characteristic Elements	Provisional Dates
Pit-and-Groove	Pits and grooves	5000 – 3000 B.C.
Great Basin Curvilinear Abstract	Circle, concentric circles, sun, chain of circles, curvilinear meander, star, snake	1000 B.C.–1500 A.D.
Great Basin Rectilinear Abstract	Rectangular grid, bird tracks, rake, cross-hatching, dots	1 – 1500 A.D.
Great Basin Representational	Mountain sheep, paw, Katchina, hand, horned human, quadruped	1 – 1500 A.D.
Great Basin Scratched	Sun, parallel lines, cross-hatching	1000 A.D.--

The Curvilinear Abstract style is outstanding in terms of the "characteristic elements" in the North Fork petroglyphs. Many circles, sun discs, curvilinear meanders, and asterisks or stars are recorded. Only the unequivocal use of a snake symbol is rare--a beautiful example some 6 feet long and clearly a rattlesnake at Site #27, but only there. [Perhaps 18 "snake symbols" in a design element tabulation of these rock carvings and fitting the definition of "a straight or wavy line and a headlike thickening at one end" (2) were noted,; however very few truly resemble a rattlesnake.] Obviously, this style has to be considered for the petroglyphs along the North Fork.

The Rectilinear Abstract style also seems appropriate. A number of rectangulr grid and cross-hatching symbols are seen, as well as bird track symbols. Dots are not seen, but the rake symbol is one of the most frequently seen in symbols of North Fork petroglyphs.

There are only a few symbols characterizing the Great Basin Representational style other than the paw or foot; but there are many of this one symbol, and especially at the two sites near early Indian campgrounds. Thus it is hard to completely dismiss this style from consideration.

The Great Basin Scratched style also can be seen in the numerous sun discs, and less frequent cross-hatching and parallel lines. However, essentially all of the petroglyphs along the North Fork appear to be pecked rather than scratched.

Thus the petroglyphs at the many sites along the North Fork of the American River have many symbols typifying the Great Basin Representational style [especially the paw], the Great Basin Rectilinear Abstract [especially the rake], and the Great Basin Curvilinear Abstract style [especially the sun disc and circles]. The style which the aborigines used along the North Fork seems to be a hybrid, perhaps drawing on Great Basin cultures but representing a still different and distinct culture.

In classifying the petroglyphs of California in a later publication, Heizer and Clewlow [3] used a different 4 "styles" which they called Great Basin, Central Sierran, Southwest Coast, and North Coast. This now seems to be more of a geographical separation, and the North Fork petroglyphs would be called Central Sierran. The book states that

> ...While it may be the case that Central Sierra petro-
> glyphs have strong affinities with other style areas,
> particularly the Great Basin petroglyph style and
> the Southern Sierra painted style, they show enough
> internal cohesion to constitute a style area of their
> own...Human figures..appear consistently in Great Basin
> pecked sites.

[By contrast, human figures are miniscule in California's Nevada County sites, very limited in Placer County sites, including those covered in this book.]

Clewlow [7] describes the revised petroglyph style as

based on segregation of the art into five major element categories. These are Human, Animal, Circle and Dot, Angular, and Curvilinear. Although many of the figures are highly stylized or abstract, if they are at all recognizable as animal or human, they are classified as such. The Circle and Dot category refers to individual elements comprised of one or more concentric circles with a dot or sphere inside, not unlike traditional "bull's eye" targets. Angular elements are geometric or subgeometric designs that consist of roughly linear segments joined at angles. Curvilinear elements are geometric or freeform designs comprised mainly of non-linear or wavy elements joined by curving lines.

I have not gone through the exercise of classifying the North Fork petroglyphs using the very limited new system of Heizer and Clewlow. There are few human symbols, very few circle-and-dot symbols; only 5 animal symbols other than the bear paw [mountain sheep, plus one obvious snake symbol] are seen. The data of Heizer and Clewlow for the Nevada County and Placer County sites they studied indicate that less than 10 percent of the symbols were human, still fewer animal, a similar paucity of circle-and-dot elements, but over 20 percent angular and over 60 percent curvilinear elements [which they suggest may be diagnostic of the Great Basin style]. For what it is worth, The North Fork petroglyph symbols also have a preponderance of curvilinear carvings.

VIII. WHY WERE THE PETROGLYPHS MADE?

   This is a natural question to ask, but the "answers" differ
among archaeologists and all of the suggestions are highly
speculative. The books by Mallery [1], by Heizer and Baumhoff
[2], and by Martineau [19] make some of these speculations on the
basis of their own observations. The additional observations
that we now have for the petroglyphs along the North Fork of the
American River can modify some of the hypotheses which
archaeologists have proposed.

   Everyone seems agreed that the petroglyphs do not represent
simply doodles or early Indian graffiti. Mallery [1] states:

   It is probable that they are not meaningless, because
   the disposition of the Indian, as he is today, is such
   that no time would be spent upon such laborious work
   without an object, and only motives of a religious or
   ceremonial nature would induce him to expend the time
   and labor necessary to accomplish such results as are
   still presented.

Later he notes that

   It is hardly likely that the work was done without
   some motive besides simple love of doing it, and it was
   well and carefully done too, showing such patience and
   doubtless consumed a good deal of time, as the tools
   were poor.

Heizer and Baumhoff [2] reach a similar conclusion and say,

   We have demonstrated that petroglyphs in Nevada and
   eastern California are evidence of the purposeful and
   rational action of prehistoric peoples. They are not
   aimless "doodling", nor are they deliberate and planned
   expressions of the artistic impulse.

   The North Fork petroglyphs can reinforce these conclusions.
Many of the rock carvings are well removed from any of the
campsites where inhabitants might have leisure time for
"doodling". Many of the rock outcroppings that would obviously
be suitable and accessible are devoid of such carvings; perhaps
they do not have the requisite vista of the mountain peaks
surrounding the North Fork. And some, especially the beautiful
petroglyph carvings above where Wabena Creek joins the American
River [Site #2], are so deeply and painstakingly cut in the
granite as to belie any likelihood of casual scratching of
graffiti by an Indian child or a bored adult.

   Are they intended for communicating some message? There is
no general agreement on the answer to this question. Mallery [1]

feels that the answer is yes. Most of his two volumes discuss possible interpretations of the symbols as efforts to communicate. He notes that some might record the passage of time, notice of visits and departures, warnings and guidance, challenges, claims, individual achievements, territorial marks, records of migration or of notable events, etc.

Martineau in his book [19] extends this idea by tying the petroglyph writing to Indian sign language. He and Mallery both give suggestive evidence for similarity of meanings of symbols in many lands, different cultures. Martineau discounts that the "mountain sheep" is a sheep at all; rather, it resembles a goat. But without logical supporting evidence, he proposes that the symbol actually represents human figures, the "sheep" symbol allowing a sense of direction or action that a stick figure of a human would not permit. [He does recognize, however, that pictures of animals also frequently may stand for tribal names, especially for those clans having animals as their totems.]

Heizer and Baumhoff [2] dispute such interpretations of the petroglyphs, stating their belief that the petroglyphs are neither a form of communicative writing nor maps. In commenting on the suggestion by Mallery that the petroglyphs may represent a thought of one person meant to be understood by another, Heizer and Baumhoff reason that each repetition of an element would have to have a distinct characteristic which remained sufficiently invariant that it would not be confused with symbols of similar form but with a different meaning. They contend that such necessary conformity was lacking in the petroglyphs they examined in Nevada. Martineau disputes this.

Our modern-day society communicates by symbols in countless ways. The profile of Alfred Hitchcock is recognizable and tells us something; signs using only symbols along the road tell us of a deer crossing; a raised hand on a sign may tell us to stop; a lighted cigarette with a diagonal cross mark means no smoking; a circle may contain a peace symbol; a cross or a swastika communicates something significant to us via a symbol. Thus it is hard to dismiss out of hand the possibility of a simple symbol communicating something significant to the prehistoric Indian.

It may never be possible to understand why one should spend the time and effort to record or communicate by making carvings on a rock. It may be easier to assess whether the site is indeed appropriate for communication to others. The North Fork petroglyph sites can all be described as being close to a campsite, to a well-used trail, or to a suitable summer hunting ground. Most of these would thus be considered suitable for communicating something to others that may follow.

<u>Why so some sites have many symbols, others only a few, and many have none?</u> The answer to this might well tell why the

51

petroglyphs were made in the first place. It has already been
mentioned that two of the petroglyph sites with large numbers of
symbols are near known campsites that must have been used over a
great many years by the early Indians, and which might then
represent the accumulation of carvings over many years. We also
have seen, however, that the appreciable number of carvings at
the two important sites on Pinehurst property do not seem to
relate to any known campground nearby.

The very fact that a large number of petroglyph sites along
the North Fork of the American River have only a few symbols, and
sometimes a single symbol, suggests that the location need not
have been selected by an Indian shaman for repeated use over the
years. I am inclined to agree with Heizer and Baumhoff [2],

Future work may lead us to some explanation of why one
site has a great abundance of petroglyphs and another
site shows only a few. Does a large number of elements
reflect a deficiency of game and the necessity of more
magic to bring it to the spot? Or does an abundance of
elements mean that there were more animals and more
hunters and, as a result, more petroglyphs? We have been
unable to suggest an answer to this problem.

Martineau [19] has his own explanation for petroglyphs
consisting of only one or two symbols. He believes they were for
communication, had to be appropriate to their locations, and
actually gave directions--Martineau calls them "locators",
directing the viewer to a larger petroglyph area, a cave, a
waterhole, etc. There are a number of examples among the North
Fork petroglyphs that indicate they, too, could be "locators",
communicating or directing. For example, Martineau's
interpretation of the "story" told by the two symbols [which he
would call "locators"] at Site #21

likely would be something like this:

The rake symbol at the left with the convex crossbar
means one should "look up above" and toward the left
for three things which the traveller may be seeking.
They will be some distance away, as shown by the long
vertical lines. The other rake symbol has a reversed or
concave crossbar, meaning one should "look down below"

and again to the left [the greater curvature] but at a shorter distance [short vertical lines] for four "things".

As it turns out, the three bedrock petroglyph "panels" at Sites #22 and #23 are indeed somewhat above and to the left [north] of Site #21. Somewhat below, closer, and to the left I have found four separate petroglyph rocks--Site #18 [really two sites, separate outcroppings, here], #19, #20. Nevertheless, such stories or instructions which Martineau cites [with the same amount of documentary evidence as that above] seem extremely far fetched.

Professor Barry Fell [28, 29] might claim that these symbols are ancient Celtic Ogam writing, where the written alphabet employs only consonants. The symbols in Ogam would spell F - S. Is there a Celtic word such as "fas"? And does it convey a realistic meaning to direct or warn the traveler? Again, there is little likelihood of this interpretation.

Is there evidence of more than one group making the petroglyphs? The answer may be yes! Although there is no difference at all in the type of site chosen, or the type of bedrock on which the petroglyphs were carved, there is some suggestive evidence of at least three and perhaps four groups having incised the symbols at the different locations along the tributaries of the North Fork. [Yet they must be of a similar culture, as evidenced by the projectile point artifacts.]

The most obvious difference is the set of rock carvings at Wabena [Site #2]. The interesting and intricate carvings there [Fig. p. 54] do not resemble any other site among the dozens of locations have petroglyphs along the North Fork tributaries; the style doesn't seem to fit the others at all. The other major difference for this set of carvings is that they are on a granitic rock that has little or no crust, in marked contrast to most of the other sites, where there is a noticeable crust in which the various symbols have been pecked and scratched [other than where basalt is used]. The Wabena petroglyphs are much deeper in the rock, and clearly required more effort to inscribe them. They also are much more obvious and visible.

A second group is suggested by symbols that are distinctly different from most sites. These locations usually only involve one or two symbols at the site, and consisting of looping lines [see Fig. p. 54]. The similarity of these symbols at Sites #26, 31, and 32 is quite evident; the glyphs resemble Arabic writing [29]. This, then, could well have been a second group of Indians making the carvings. But it also could merely represent a special type of message, since the other three glyphs at Site #26 are not different from some seen at a number of locations.

Some Unusual Symbols at Site #2 near Wabena

Similar Symbols with Looping Lines

Site #31

Site #26

Site #32

At Site #22 we see another set of carvings that are rather different. The numerous wavy, winding lines are quite distinctive and not found elsewhere. One of these waving lines is up to nine feet long, and beautifully done. This is the one site where mapping is suggested [this is discussed in detail on p. 59 et seq]; it can relate solely to this location, a particular ceremonial use, or [less likely] can suggest that it was inscribed by a quite different group of prehistoric Indians.

A possible fourth group making the petroglyphs would be identified with the massive sets of carvings at Site #6 and at Site #27. These two sites have very similar types of symbols, each has more than two hundred individual carvings, and each is close by a major prehistoric Indian camp adjoining the old Indian migratory trail paralleling the river. The likelihood is that many more individuals made the carvings at these sites, but not that a different tribal group is involved.

Hundreds of projectile points have been found around camp areas near the two major petroglyph sites, #6 and #27. Interestingly, the significant set of carvings at Sites #22 and #23 have not had any artifacts associated with them. The Pinehurst families have not found projectile points in the neighborhood of these sites, in marked contrast to Sites #6 and #27.

It would not be surprising to find two different aboriginal groups making the North Fork rock carvings, quite probably at different periods of time. [The Martis Complex covers a long period of perhaps well over 1000 years.] A parallel instance is cited for two sets of petroglyphs in southeastern Nevada; Heizer and Hester [5] mention that two sites there are only 33 miles apart, but are "quite distinct stylistically".

The current limited evidence is that the petroglyphs at Wabena [#2] were carved by a different group and at a different time, but that the remainder of the rock carvings in the upper North Fork watershed were all incised by the same prehistoric Indian group--probably the peoples of the Martis Complex.

IX. WHAT DO THE PETROGLYPH SYMBOLS MEAN?

This is usually the first question asked, one that everyone [including the archaeologist] is interested in. It is a question that scientists have grappled with for over a hundred years, with no real answers.

It should be noted that essentially all of the symbols appearing on the rocks in the North Fork watershed are just that--symbols, rather than true depictions of humans, animals, insects, plants. A few "stick figures" clearly represent humans. A tiny few "mountain sheep" represent four-footed animals. Many "bear paws" do indeed seem to represent paws. But a glance at the design elements listed on p. 37 tells us that obscure symbolism must account for most of the carvings. Yet they are repeated, and must have had meaning to the prehistoric tribes there.

Grant [20] states a truism, that any understanding of the petroglyphs must be based on some knowledge of their creators. This is why we have spent so much time with the question, Who made these petroglyphs? When were they made? Why were they made? Knowing something of this, interpretations of some of the petroglyph symbols may be possible.

What might the early Indian wish to record? It is easy to think of a half-dozen types of events or other things that might be considered as significant and worth recording in rock carvings.

a] **A record of astronomical events or observations.** These could encompass an eclipse, meteor, nova, constellations, Venus or Polaris, or the summer solstice or autumn equinox. [In the high Sierra, the winter solstice and the spring equinox would not be observed because the Indians would have left the mountains for a more hospitable climate during those months.]

Hudson and Underhay [21] cite many instances where such recordings presumably are found in rock art in southern California. Unique use of symbols, such as the spiral, has been shown by archaeologists to have been employed by the prehistoric Indian to precisely predict or determine a solstice or equinox of the sun; this is particularly seen in the southwestern states and in Mexico.

Kroeber [4] writes:

Astronomical knowledge not directly used in time reckoning was slight in northern and central California. The planets were too difficult to trouble with, except for Venus when it was the morning star. The Pleiades are the constellation most frequently mentioned, and seem to

have had a designation among every tribe...Orion's belt
is probably recognized with the next greatest frequency,
and then possibly Ursa Major. There are some references
to Polaris as the immovable star. The Milky Way is known
everywhere, and quite generally to be of some conse-
quence...

Wilson and Towne [9] noted that among the Nisenan, stars for
the most part were not known, but they recognized and named the
Big Dipper, morning and evening stars [Venus].

Heizer and Baumhoff [2] feel that the interest in
astronomical phenomena evidenced by the early peoples in the
Southwest and southern California is not shared by tribes further
north, noting that

...Great Basin tribes exhibit decidedly less interest
in the cosmic phenomena. Judging from the relatively
slight interest by native tribes of Nevada in astronomical phenomena, we might expect that these would not
appear prominently in petroglyph designs.

Kroeber [4] concurs.

The American Ephemeris and Nautical Almanac gives the
azimuth [sun's compass direction] at sunrise near Reno as 57°, or
33° N of E at the summer solstice. Two petroglyph symbols at
Donner [Site #1] seemed to suggest an orientation toward this
angle. In June 1980 I was there before the sunrise to observe
this. The markings did indeed aim at the rising sun as it emerged
over the rock peak by the Observation Point on Old Highway 40,
but this most likely was fortuitous. Somewhat similar types of
symbols elsewhere bear no relation or orientation to the summer
solstice azimuth.

Close examination of the many hundreds of symbols on the
North Fork petroglyphs brings a tiny handful that might be
interpreted [by modern man] as depicting an astronomical event:
eclipse of the sun possibly at Sites #6 and #27; a comet at Site
#6; and a meteor [or Venus?] at Site #22 carvings. No glyphs
depict a moon crescent. Generally, one can say that unless very
obscure symbolism was used, the people making the North Fork
petroglyphs did not use them to signify astronomical events.

b] A **record** of **environmental events.** These might be the
migration of the deer, spring floods, rain, lightning,
earthquakes, fire, an unusual storm. It is possible that the
parallel wavy lines in some rake symbols [p. 46] and the
beautiful wavy lines that are present in the symbol at Site #28
may relate to some of these environmental effects. Also, one
could rationalize that lightning is depicted in the jagged
rectangular lines such as seen at Sites #1, 3, 4, 14, 27, and 33.

But if so,, it is more likely that it will be related to religious-magical-ceremonial significance or a moiety totem.

c] **A count, such as a recording of passage of time.** Modern man when isolated and without a calendar will make a mark to record the passage of days. The rake symbol is very suggestive of such a marking of the days or months [moons] at a camp, or even of the years of returning to the hunting grounds. Indeed, perhaps a dozen of the rakes have a crossbar noticeably extended well beyond the vertical lines [see p. 38, E, F, L], which can suggest that a continuing tabulation was anticipated, with more lines to be added subsequently.

Regarding the possibility of a petroglyph calendar, Kroeber, however, observed [4]:

> The California Indian did not record the passage of long intervals of time...Tallies seem not to have been kept, and no sticks notched annually have been reported ...Probably every tribe, however, had a system of measuring time within the year. This was by the universally known method of naming and reckoning lunations within the round of the seasons.

Maravillas Gortner has translated an important treatise by S.G. Reyna [22] on the Cave of Pileta near Ronda, Malaga, Spain. In this booklet there is a photo of some of the Paleolithic drawings on the walls of this cave, and some could easily match up with symbols on Indian petroglyphs in the Sierras. I have visited this cave; it has beautiful paintings on the wall made during the last ice age. One of the striking symbols [to one who has seen the prehistoric Indian petroglyphs in California] is the rake--identical with many seen in the rock carvings half-way around the world and perhaps ten thousand years later. Conceivably both aborigines used this as a type of calendar to mark the passage of time.

d] **A recording of a geographical area; a map.** Heizer and Baumhoff [2] discount any possibility that the petroglyphs function as maps, though Mallery [1] thought they might. Yet Heizer [4] admits that although the California Indians may not have consciously thought of maps, when asked for directions they often could and would draw a map on the earth. He cites an account in 1844 in Nevada where the Indians made a drawing on the ground showing the Truckee River issuing from Lake Tahoe, 3 or 4 days distant, with the Sierra beyond it, and still further two major rivers [possibly the Sacramento, American, or Feather Rivers]. The directions indicated were also correct. Heizer stated that the Indians' mapping technique was aboriginal, but adds that there is nothing remarkable in these maps scratched in the sands, since primitive peoples throughout the world can make charts of areas known to them. In the use of a series of trails by the California Indians involved in tribal trade, simple maps might have a functional use.

Two possibilities were considered in my detailed study of the North Fork petroglyphs. One is that some of the angular lines that were carved might relate to the mountain peaks. When these symbols were examined at the site, none appeared to depict the ridge skyline viewed from the watershed of the North Fork.

The other mapping possibility was suggested by the unusual, extensive, meandering, and often interconnecting lines at Site #22. The carvings in several of the drawings shown in the Appendix are most provocative in suggesting a mapping function.

[1] Perhaps the most clear-cut of the "map" glyphs is the meandering, wavy line which appears on the rock carvings at Site #22 shown in Fig. p. 60. In the small circle at the top, the symbol suggests a lake, and there is a long wavy line extending from it. When a tracing of a photo of this symbol is superimposed on a tracing from a contour map of the upper watershed of the North Fork of the American River, one can see a strikingly close resemblance. The wavy line corresponds to the presently recognized Old Indian Migratory Trail [or a hunting trail paralleling it] running from Mountain Meadow Lake near the Sierra crest down several miles along the North Fork. The petroglyph sites found near this stretch of the river are shown; they clearly follow this suggested trail.

This petroglyph appears to be a remarkably well-executed map incised in the granite. Yet this one example is not enough to refute previously expressed opinions that the petroglyphs do not serve as maps.

[2] Another prominent symbol at Site #22 includes large wavy lines that diverge and later converge, and have a connecting wavy link [Fig. p. 61]. This clearly cannot be representing streams, for the connecting linkage would be unexplainable then. Conceivably the lines could be mapping hunting trails used by the prehistoric Indians, in which case the connecting link would be a trail marking a passage from one major trail to a second trail. The contour map of the area suggests that the lower line in the figure shown may be a hunting trail paralleling the migratory Indian trail along the south side of the North Fork of the American River. The upper line could be a trail rising from the valley to a rocky ridge and plateau, and on through the woods to a fabulous open granite shelf called Inspiration Point [Site #16]. It could then go on and gradually descend to join the Indian trail at the river past the Chickering camp. The connecting link on the symbol might be a trail from Inspiration Point dropping down directly over a series of exposed rocky shelves, to go across the river and join the other trail at Site #22, where this "map" is incised.

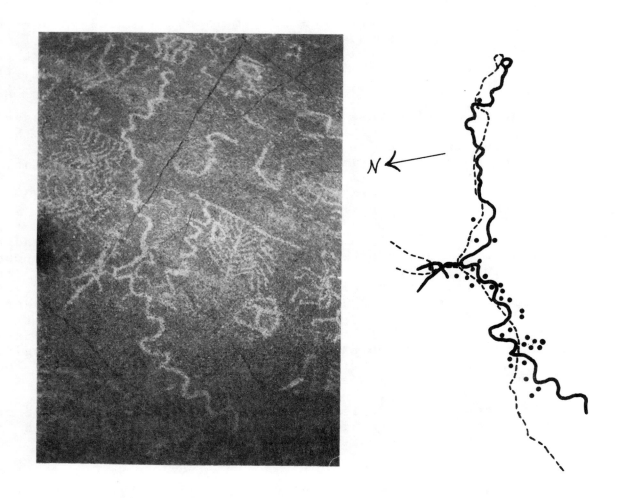

Map #1? A tracing of the Site #22 symbol in the
photo is superimposed on the river (dashed line) as traced
from a contour map. Identified petroglyph sites along the
river are noted.

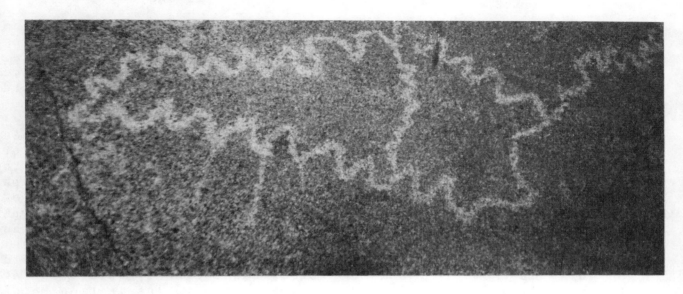

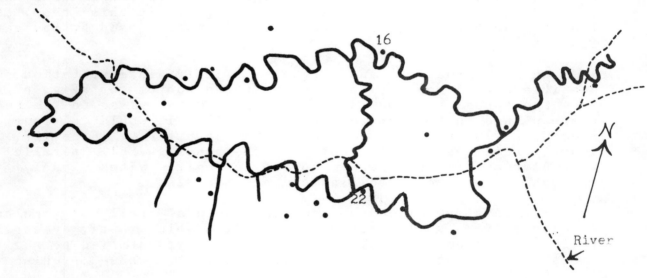

Map #2? A tracing of the photo of this symbol at
Site #22 is fitted over identified petroglyph sites. The
North Fork of the American River and a tributary are shown
in the dashed lines.

This would seem to fit the known petroglyph sites near the trails, and only would have to assume existence of a connecting trail about where a very recent path was blazed by Cedars people. In 1982 I hiked this presumed connecting trail, and found a nice basalt Martis point midway along the trail while going toward Site #22.

[3] Still another grouping of meandering lines is also seen among the symbols of the Site #22 petroglyphs. When a tracing of a photo of this symbol is placed on a contour map of the North Fork region, there is a reasonable agreement of the petroglyph sites found in the area with either of two different sets of trails which could be represented in the carving. The petroglyph and stream locations are superimposed on tracings of the petroglyph photo in Fig. p. 63. One possible and logical interpretation is at the upper right. The trail on the left would be going up from the river to follow Cedar Creek, while that at the right would go up the rocky ridge and on to Inspiration Point [Site #16], a trail just described in [2]. In this case, the loop at the bottom would approximate a campsite used by the early Indians.

An alternative and equally likely interpretation of possible trail maps is that shown at the bottom of Fig. p. 63. Here the upper trail would proceed up from the river to the rocky plateau and on to Inspiration Point. Then it would continue on from Site #16 to again come down to the river by Site #27. The lower trail again would represent the hunting trail paralleling the American River. Here also the petroglyph sites closely fit the outline of the symbol incised at Site #22.

If this symbol on the rock is indeed a trail map, either interpretation would represent a reasonable route, generally follows the contour map, and closely fits identified petroglyph sites that must be along trails used by these prehistoric Indians.

[4] A fourth meandering set of lines suggesting 3 different "trails" is seen in the photograph of yet another petroglyph symbol at Site #22 [Fig. p. 64]. When a tracing of this symbol is placed on a contour map, logical trails again can be identified. The upper line might represent a trail ascending up on the north side of Cedar Creek. The middle trail would go up the rocky ridge from the river and continue on through the woods to meet the other trails at Site #15. Finally, the trail represented by the wavy line at the right of the figure would descend past Inspiration Point [Site #16] to Site #22 [where the symbol appears] and then follow on westward along the trail on the south side of the American River.

62

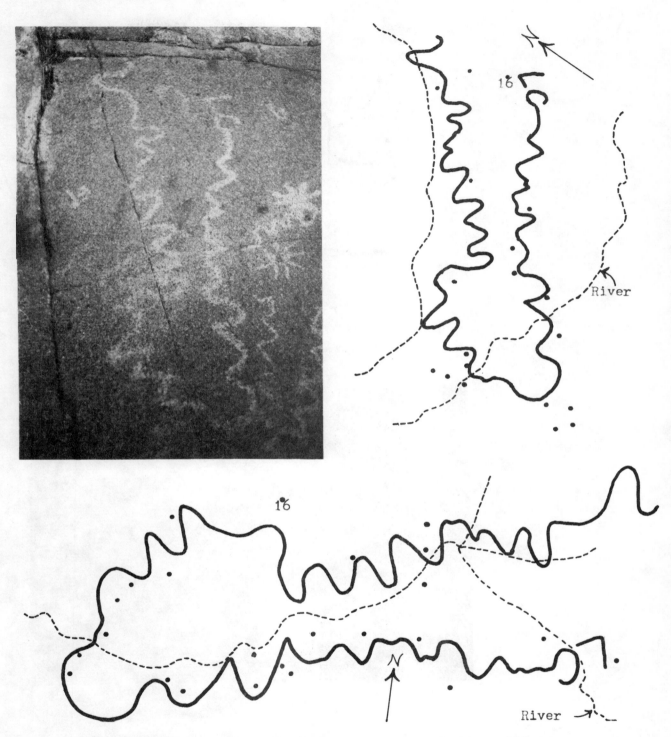

Map #3? Two possible interpretations of the symbol at
Site #22 are shown. Tracings of the symbol are superimposed on
two alternative contour map tracings of petroglyph sites and
the North Fork of the American River and tributaries.

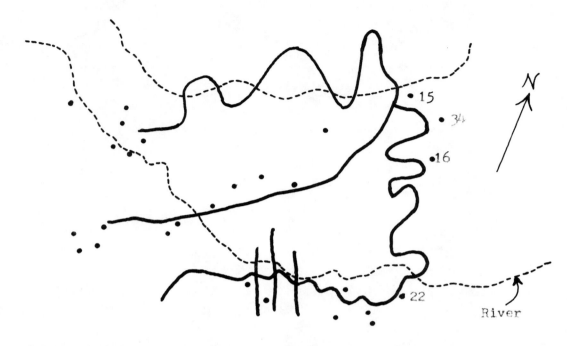

Map #4? The tracing of the photo of this symbol
at Site #22 is placed over a contour map tracing of a creek
and the North Fork of the American River (dashed lines).
Identified petroglyph locations are shown.

Interestingly, this "map" led to discovery of petroglyph Site #34. I had reasoned that there should be some evidence to support the interpretation of a previously unrecognized trail between Inspiration Point [Site #16] and Cedar Creek [Site #15]. When I subsequently hiked through this area, I did indeed find a series of rocky domes, one of which had several rock carvings on it [Site #34]. The "trail" did indeed exist!

[5] And there is still a fifth line on the rock carvings at Site #22 that may well represent a trail map, although categorized as a "snake symbol". This is a beautiful, long line carved in the granite and extending for some 9 feet in length [Fig. p. 66]. The lake-like oval at the head is strongly suggestive of Mountain Meadow Lake, the headwater of the North Fork, and the long line suggests the American River down to Log Cabin Creek, looping up that creek as the tail of the carving. This is the one "map" that seems to be stylized; each of the others has very wavy lines as trails, but this is only gently undulating. Nevertheless, it is a reasonable [but stylized] depiction of the very part of the river where most of the petroglyphs are found.

The conclusion from these five meandering line symbols on a single petroglyph panel is that they are likely maps of Indian trails, and surprisingly well drawn in fitting the land and the various petroglyph sites, considering that they were incised in the granite some thousands of years ago, by an aboriginal, stone-age people.

Since identifiable trail maps are only seen at this one location [Site #22] among the dozens of sites along the North Fork of the American River, it is reasonable to ask, why this particular area. My belief is that here is the focal point for the "hunting magic" of these peoples--where the shaman could invoke success to the hunt, and be able to include all of the hunting trails depicted in the rock carvings. Nearly all of these trails are visible in the sweeping panorama viewed from this petroglyph rock, which forms a lofty and imposing platform dropping sharply down on the north to the river perhaps 150 feet below. It is just the sort of prominent pedestal which a shaman might choose for magic incantations--and inscriptions.

Clewlow [7] notes that some of the petroglyph sites in the Central Sierra might have reflected tribal boundary marks. Thus this too can support the possibility that a geographical area may be recorded in petroglyph carvings on the rocks [though this is unlikely in the limited hunting ground areas of the North Fork unless it was used by a single tribe of the Martis Imdians].

e] A record of a personal or cultural nature. These might be to record a success in a hunt, or in warfare; a marking of a campsite; basket-type art, or another art expression; a tribal

65

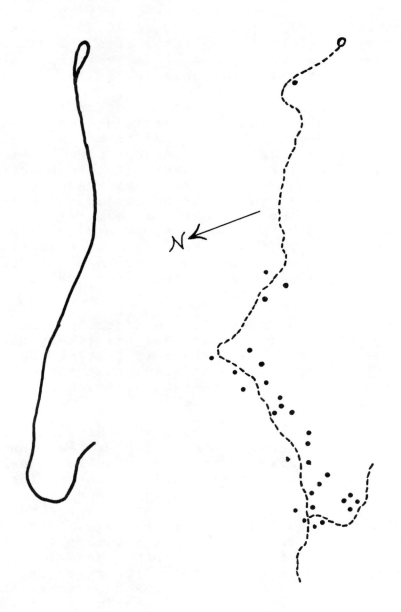

Map #5? The tracing at the left was made from a
photograph of the 9-foot long symbol at Site #22. The figure
at the right was made by tracing a contour map of the North
Fork of the American River and the petroglyph locations near
it. A tributary is also shown.

"totem" symbol. Or, naturally, graffiti.

The various possibilities are almost impossible to interpret with any conviction, but most do not seem to be very promising. For example, Wilson and Towne [9] mention that for the Nisenan, snowshoes consisted of a circular hoop of willow or redbud with two cross-pieces tied with sinew. Can one extrapolate this to a petroglyph symbol of a circle or oval with two cross markings [as seen in several petroglyph sites] and interpret the markings as snowshoes? Very unlikely.

Perhaps the idea that various Indian totemic "moiety" symbols might be recorded is worth further examination. Mallery [1] pointed out that from the earliest times peoples have used symbols or emblems [totems] to indicate their tribes or clans. He goes on to say,

As most Indian tribes were zootheistic, the object of their devotion was generally an animal--e.g., an eagle, a panther, a buffalo, a bear, a deer, a racoon, a snake, or a fish, but sometimes was one of the winds, a celestial body, or other impressive object or phenomenon.

I have previously referred [p. 7] to some of the many totems used by the Miwok Indians [and perhaps other tribes as well], suggesting that their moiety totemic characters might relate to petroglyph symbols of bear paws, sun discs, stars, rain, etc. Mallery [1] and Grant [20] mention petroglyphs in Arizona where various symbols are repeated many times; an Indian chief explained that when each Indian stopped at the spring there, he would draw his totem, the symbol, presumably, of his clan and moiety. In discussing the bear paw symbol, Grant says that this grizzly bear paw motif was used by some tribes as a clan symbol.

One can speculate that the frequent use of the bear paw in the rock carvings might reflect a totem for a family of the "land moiety"; the subdivisions on the palm of the paw might personalize the symbol. The wavy lines frequently seen in other petroglyph symbols might be a totem for a "water moiety" family.

f] A record of religious or magic or ceremonial significance. This is the one favored by Heizer and his associates. They consider the petroglyphs as part of the magical or ritual aspect of hunting. Indeed, they [2] reach

...the conclusion that the actual making of petroglyphs was a magical or ritual act, and that there existed a powerful taboo against making petroglyphs in places, for purposes, and by persons other than those directly associated with the hunt.

A few glyphs of human stick figures suggest some ceremonial meaning. The one at Site #46 along the Yuba River [p. 43] with the human apparently holding two symbols appears to have such a significance, and is provocative because the chevron symbol appears alone elsewhere [especially at Site #27--pp. 141, 149, 152] and the connected-circle-with-rays symbol appears alone at Sites # 1 [p.84], #15 [p.117], and #35 [p.162] along the North Fork watershed. Other human figures that appear to be holding something include those at Site #42 [p.165] and at Site #27 [pp. 142, 148]. Another at Site #27 [p. 138] suggests that a high chieftan may be depicted with a ceremonial, fringed robe. Does this imply that a funeral was held there for one of the important leaders of the tribe?

One might readily extend the "totemic character" idea discussed above to include the ceremonial or mystic concept or symbolism of the shamans. As noted on p. 8 of this writing, Kroeber [4] felt that three important shamans of historic tribes in the Sierra foothills were the weather or rain shaman, the rattlesnake shaman, and the grizzly bear shaman. Were these also part of the ritual-religious beliefs of their ancestors, the Martis peoples? What might their symbols then depict?

The rain doctor might use one or more of symbols A-D, p. 69. The dark basalt constituting part of the symbol in A-C suggests a rain cloud, and the rays extend from only part of the circular area; they do not appear to convey a sun symbol, though they might indeed show the sun extending from behind a rain cloud. These and many more basaltic, rain-like symbols are to be seen at Site #27, but only a single symbol at two or three other sites uses the basalt in this manner [and far less effectively] and might similarly be interpreted as rain. Symbol D is a complex and large symbol, and the oval includes two elements suggesting a rain from a cloud. Does this--or the others--constitute a rain doctor symbol, and indicate the presence of the rain or weather shaman at this site?

The grizzly bear doctor very possibly has his mark in the Symbol F [p. 69] also at Site #27. It is unique [compare Fig. p. 40], the only such symbol among more than a thousand carvings in petroglyphs along the North Fork and its tributaries. Thus, while the stylized "bear paws" seen in dozens of locations may well be family moiety totems, this single grizzly paw symbol is more likely to reflect the presence of the important bear shaman.

And also at Site #27 is the large and well-done depiction of a rattlesnake [E]. This symbol [again, showing the snake's rattles and the only such one anywhere] is even more certainly associated with the ceremonial shamans, this time the rattlesnake doctor.

Possible Shaman Symbols in the Rock at Site #27

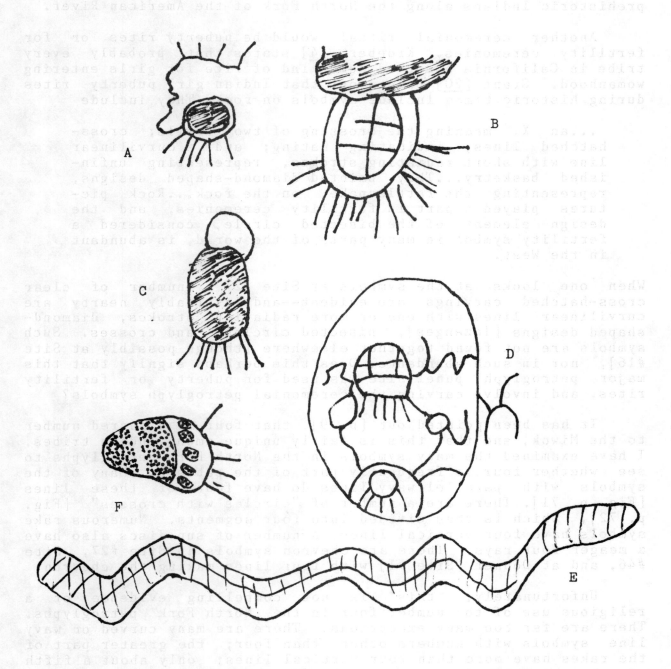

The interpretation of these few symbols as relating to the tribal shamans seems reasonable--and clearly suggests a significance of this particular site in the summer life of the prehistoric Indians along the North Fork of the American River.

Another ceremonial ritual would be puberty rites or for fertility ceremonies. Kroeber [4] states that probably every tribe in California observed some kind of rite for girls entering womanhood. Grant [20] points out that Indian girl puberty rites during historic times include symbols on rocks.They include

> ...an X, meaning the crossing of two trails; cross-hatched lines, indicating mating; and a curvilinear line with short radiating strokes, representing unfinished basketry...They painted diamond-shaped designs, representing the rattlesnake, on the rock...Rock pictures played a part in fertility ceremonies, and the design element of the bisected circle, considered a fertility symbol in many parts of the world, is abundant in the West.

When one looks at the symbols at Site #27 a number of clear cross-hatched carvings are evident--and invariably nearby are curvilinear lines with one or more radiating strokes, diamond-shaped designs [lozenges], bisected circles, and crosses. Such symbols are not found together elsewhere [though possibly at Site #16], nor in such abundance. Does this perhaps signify that this major petroglyph panel site was used for puberty or fertility rites, and involve carving the ceremonial petroglyph symbols?

It has been pointed out [p. 9] that four is a sacred number to the Miwok, and that this is fairly unique among Indian tribes. I have examined the many symbols in the North Fork petroglyphs to see whether four is frequently part of the pattern. Many of the symbols with parallel wavy lines do have four of these lines [Fig. p. 71]. There are a number of "circles with crosses" [Fig. p. 72], which is thus divided into four segments. Numerous rake symbols have four vertical lines. A number of sun discs also have a meager four rays. There are chevron symbols at Site #27, Site #46, and at Donner [Site #1] with four lines making the chevron.

Unfortunately, this is not compelling evidence of a religious use of the number four in the North Fork petroglyphs. There are far too many exceptions. There are many curved or wavy line symbols with numbers other than four; the greater part of the rakes have more than four vertical lines; only about a fifth of the paws have four claws; the same is true for the sun disc symbols.

Wavy or Curved Lines in Symbols (Suggestive of
Water--a Miwok Totem) and Numbering Four (a Miwok
Ritual Number)

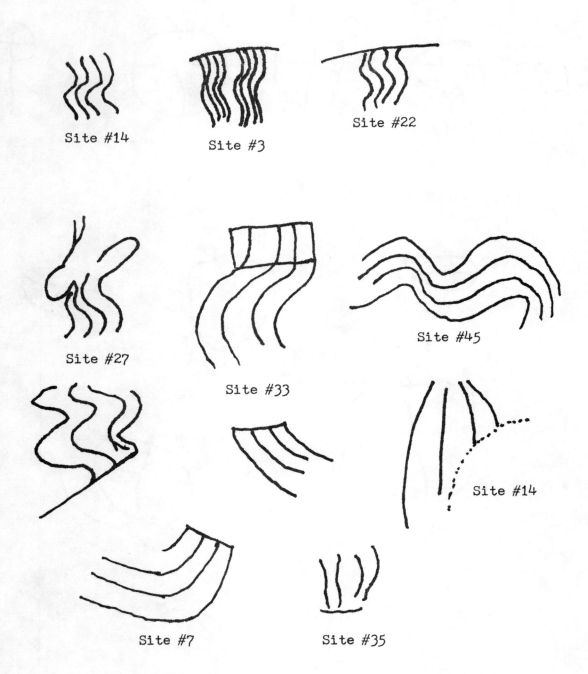

Site #14

Site #3

Site #22

Site #27

Site #33

Site #45

Site #14

Site #7

Site #35

"Circles" with Crosses as Symbols

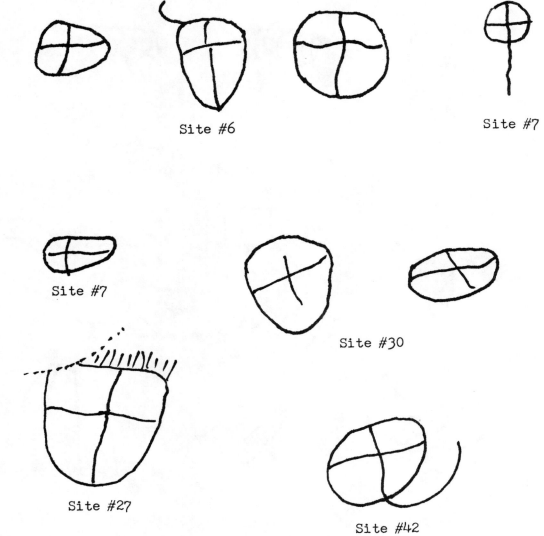

Site #6

Site #7

Site #7

Site #30

Site #27

Site #42

Other types of symbolism have been looked for, since they have been inferred elsewhere. An example: the Sierra Miwok have the

        ...idea of the earth as floating in an ocean with the
        sky dome arching over it all like a gigantic bowl [7].

One can easily [but probably erroneously] relate this to some petroglyph symbols that have been observed along the North Fork.

On the other hand, one or two symbols on North Fork petroglyphs do possibly relate to a known religious Indian depiction of either their "thunderbird" or a supernatural being. Some of the glyphs depicted in Fig. p. 74 suggest a supernatural being [though that at Site #5 could equally well be depicting a hunter camouflaged with antlers and deer hide, known to be a ruse of Indians approaching a deer in historic times].

The several symbols with numerous hair-like markings at Wabena [Site #1, Fig. p. 75] suggest at least some similarity to a presumed bird [thunderbird?] motif depicted in the book by Hudson and Underhay [21]. Yet the latter symbol was presumably painted by Chumash Indians and many hundreds of miles further south in California.

g] **Instructions, perhaps via Indian sign language.** This is suggested with some vigor by Martineau [19], but is supported by anecdotal evidence only. There is little or no evidence to be found in the North Fork petroglyphs suggesting that the symbols might be meant to instruct or direct or guide or warn someone other than the carver.

Can even the simple symbols that occur frequently be interpreted? The discussion previously has highlighted the many problems of identifying what a symbol meant to the one who incised it in the rock some thousands of years before the White man came, without its meaning being continued in tribal legends or tales, and even before the Indian tribes in historical times hunted in this area and became aware of the petroglyphs.

The bear paw symbol--would it be a family or tribal totem, a religious symbol, a shaman totem,, a warning, a magic symbol to give strength, a mark of a successful hunt for bear? Why the many lines across the palm, and the variable number of claws?

The rake symbol--would it imply a calendar, or recording of events? Why the wavy versus straight versus curved versus foreshortened lines?

The sun disc symbol--does it signify a sun, a moon, a star, a nova, or a rainstorm, when the rays are only on one segment of the circle, and may be wavy?

Possible Supernatural Beings or Thunderbirds

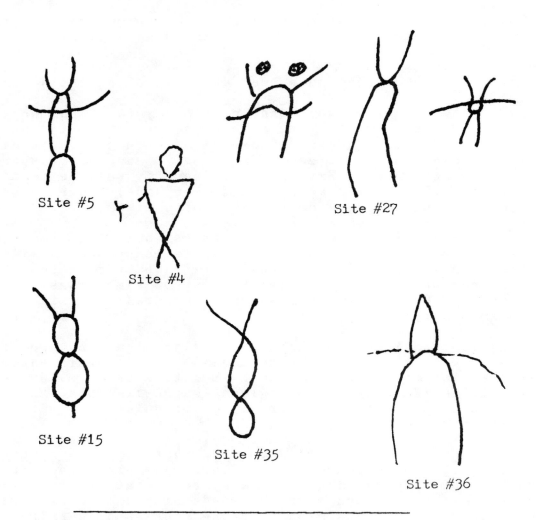

Site #5

Site #4

Site #27

Site #15

Site #35

Site #36

Compare with Dakota Indian Thunderbird Symbols (1, p. 483)

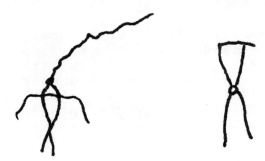

Comparison of Symbols at Site #2
with One in Ventura County

Symbols at Site #2

Presumed Bird Motif
from Ventura County (21, p. 91)

Why [in a very few symbols] is the entire enclosed space in the symbol pecked or scratched out [such as at Sites #22, 27, and 46]? What interpretations should be made for the appreciable number of symbols that are using basaltic intrusions in the granite as an important part of a petroglyph symbol [see Fig. p. 34], as seen at Sites #5, 6, 14, 16, 22, and 27, and with numerous ones at Donner [Site #1]? The major petroglyph analysts fail to even note this, but Martineau [19] does recognize that

> ...some symbols followed cracks in the rocks, ended, or were purposely placed at the rock's edge. Natural holes or other rock features were often embodied in the makeup of the symbol.

These questions cannot be answered at this time, and may never be. Even speculation is just that, without any reasonable corrobatory or documentary evidence.

Nevertheless, I am inclined to agree with Heizer and Hester [5] when they say,

> It is most likely, it seems to us, that as different styles developed and spread, the design elements which comprise each style had a name and meaning. What the "snake" or "dumbell" or "grid" or "rake" designs signified in their makers' minds we admit we do not know, but at the same time we do believe that they probably stood for some specific item, or idea, or concept.

They considered that the widespread occurrence of many of the symbols in petroglyphs is suggestive evidence that the meaning was retained.

The facts, the suggestive evidence implied from them, the reasoning from the culture of the Indians who occupied this region in historic times do allow me to make an educated guess about the significance and/or meaning of a tiny few of the petroglyph symbols I have found along the North Fork of the American River.

It seems unlikely that the many more stylistic renditions of the "bear paw" symbol is the totem of a "bear shaman". It varies too much, such as in the lines in the paws dividing the palm pad into a number of sections. A more likely interpretation of many symbols is that they reflect the family totem within a moiety. As noted on p. 8, such totems easily could be variations of the bear paw, the deer hoof, a snake, a sun disc, a star, rain or water via wavy parallel lines, a tadpole [a circle with a wavy tail?], etc. Interestingly, the bear paw symbol is the most frequent at places near major campsites--three-fourths of these symbols along the upper reaches of the North Fork are near these early Indian campsites, Sites # 6 and #27. This supports the totem hypothesis.

There are many so-called "bear paw" symbols--but only one is distinctly different, and constitutes a more accurate version of a grizzly bear paw print. There are many snake-like symbols--but again, only one is distinctly different, clearly and fairly accurately a representation of a large rattlesnake. Both of these occur only once, at Site #27. As previously noted, these defensibly can be interpreted as the totems of the "bear shaman" and the "rattlesnake shaman". One can argue that the presence of a "rattlesnake shaman" or of a "rain doctor" is somewhat unlikely despite petroglyph symbols that could be appropriate since neither of these shamans might have a prime function in a summer hunt at the elevation of the upper reaches of the North Fork [unless an entire tribal camp from the foothills moved to the mountains in the summer]; at 6000 foot elevation or more, rattlesnakes are no problem, and the Sierra sumer hunting time is quite free of rain [though it may have differed in 1500 B.C. times]; indeed, rain is not sought when hunting. But all shamans have more general, ceremonial duties and are useful in the tribal functioning.

Discovery of an Indian basalt quarry adjacent to the carvings at Site #32 temporarily posed a possible explanation of a particular glyph. Did the looping lines refer to the basalt quarry, or its "ownership"? On p. 54 one can see the similarity to the glyph at Site #31. Unfortunately, a survey near that site showed the complete absence there of any suitable basalt for the Indian's toolmaking. The hypothesis for interpreting these glyphs was not supported.

X.DO THE PETROGLYPHS BY THE NORTH FORK CHANGE ANY EXISTING
THEORIES?

Yes, and add a few new ideas in the process.

Heizer and his associates proposed that the petroglyphs were
magico-religious symbols associated with communal hunts and near
game trails. Everything about the North Fork petroglyphs would
agree with this, but it no longer needs to be qualified by
referring to group hunting, such as for antelope or buffalo in
desert areas of the Great Basin. The taking of game along the
North Fork of the American River was unlikely to be a group
event, and much more likely to be done by individual Indians. Yet
the many rock carvings along the game trails attest to the
belief of the early Indian in the efficacy of the petroglyph
carvings.

The North Fork petroglyphs also appear to differ from rock
carvings at other locations by having some fairly clear-cut and
well-drawn maps of the trails used by the summer hunters. Others
have discounted the idea that the prehistoric Indian rock
carvings included maps, but the Site #22 petroglyph panel
certainly includes trail maps.

Four other findings about the North Fork petroglyph sites
make them somewhat unique. One is that each site is at a
location that has a fine view of the magnificent major mountain
peaks surrounding the upper reaches of the North Fork of the
American River; here it seems to be obligatory in the choice of a
rock outcropping for use in making a petroglyph carving. Yet this
aesthetic aspect is lacking in the Indian petroglyph sites
alsewhere.

A second finding is that the petroglyphs never are carved on
a vertical or cliff face, or on a boulder. Only bedrock is used,
and usually a nearly horizontal surface of the rock. Again, this
is in marked contrast to rock carvings elsewhere.

Another point about the sites along the North Fork of the
American River is their frequency--there are literally dozens of
individual petroglyph sites within an area of only a few square
miles. And many show only a tiny few symbols or glyphs.
Petroglyphs recorded elsewhere in Nevada and California appear to
have many symbols, and they seem to be restricted to only one or
perhaps two sites within a limited geographic area. Or is it that
rocks with only two or three weathered and indistinct symbols
will not be very evident to the passerby and thus likely would be
overlooked unless an intensive search was made?

A fourth point also suggests the uniqueness of the North
Fork petroglyphs. Heizer and Baumhoff [2] called attention to the
lack of petroglyphs on the Tahoe side of the Central Sierra. I

studied the acres of beautiful, pink-crusted granite outcroppings in Emigrant Canyon and Coldstream Canyon on the east side of the Pacific Crest Trail past Anderson and Lincoln Peaks. No rock carvings could be found. The North Fork watershed seems to have a special relationship in attracting the Martis Complex Indians to peck their petroglyph symbols.

The hypothesis of Heizer and his associates that the petroglyphs were discontinued in late prehistoric times because they had been associated with group hunting, and a change in hunting methods may have made the magic of a petroglyph unnecessary, may now be modified by the findings from the North Fork petroglyphs. The discontinuing of the ritual of pecking petroglyphs was not related to a change toward hunting singly, since that was always the likely method in the mountainous area along the North Fork of the American River. But a change in the method of killing game must have occurred as the bow and arrow were introduced and widely adopted by tribes in the region. This might well have resulted in the finding that other desirable hunting areas were now feasible. Thus it is possible that the region around the petroglyphs thereafter became used only minimally. At any rate, the discontinued use of rock art coincides with the period of the first use of the bow and arrow in California.

The circumstantial evidence brought together in this study also suggests that many of the symbols appearing in the North Fork petroglyphs may be totems identifying a family moiety.

There is now fairly good evidence that the hunters along the North Fork of the American River were of the Martis Complex, and that the North Fork petroglyph sites represent still another summer hunting ground typifying that ancient Indian civilization.

This intensive regional study is the first to unequivocally relate a petroglyph [and indeed, a petroglyph style] with a specific, truly ancient, prehistoric Indian tribal group. The Martis peoples made these petroglyphs, and the "Central Sierran" style [3] typifies their rock carvings. Indeed, this additionally provides good evidence for dating the Central Sierran petroglyph style at approximately 1700-1000 B.C., based on radiocarbon dating of numerous Martis sites.

This thus is also the first evidence that the Martis Complex Indians made extensive use of petroglyph inscribing. This knowledge now may help in interpreting some of the glyphs, and adds another aspect to our meager knowledge of their lifestyle, beliefs, and culture. It also may explain the discontinuance of this rock art form, since the flaked artifacts around the Central Sierra that are associated with the Martis Complex also phased out by 800 A.D.

XI. WHERE HAS ALL THIS BROUGHT US?

Many different threads have been brought together and woven into a more complete fabric. As these threads joined others, a pattern emerged. This pattern--this picture--brings us significant insight into the rock art carvings as well as the early peoples in the Central Sierra wilderness who made them.

Within a relatively few square miles of Placer County land in California bordering the upper reaches of the North Fork of the American River, 46 prehistoric Indian petroglyph sites have been identified. Only 2 of these sites had been identified previously. The North Fork petroglyphs have well over 1700 individual carvings on about 80 bedrock granite outcroppings. Each symbol was sketched on a 1:10 scale, and each site was identified and recorded for altitude, for location by compass triangulation, and description of the locality and its view was noted.

All of the petroglyphs were pecked on flat or gently sloping bedrock, nearly always of granite. Some of the carvings appear in or otherwise use the dark gray basalt areas often occurring in the granite. No petroglyph appears on boulders or cliff faces.

Only a very few of the sites have extensive petroglyph carvings. Indeed, a unique feature is that the majority of the sites have very few carvings in the rock; some have only one or two symbols. But every site has a view of one or more of the major peaks around the headwaters and upper watershed of the North Fork.

The pattern of the sites over several miles of the North Fork of the American River and its tributaries suggests that the petroglyph sites follow trails used by the prehistoric Indians [perhaps ancestors of the Nisenan or Southern Maidu, but possibly of either the Washo or the Miwok] in hunting game. The prehistoric Indians were almost certainly of the "Martis Complex", occupying lands near Lake Tahoe on the eastern side of the Sierra Nevada range and along the trail routes over the mountain passes and down to the foothills on the western slope.

There is strong evidence that trail maps were included in the petroglyph carvings. These may have been less for communicating with or guiding other hunters than for their religious or ceremonial significance.

The petroglyphs were probably made some 3000 years ago. This is suggested by several tenuous bits of reasoning, but primarily by the radiocarbon dating of a number of campsites of the Martis Complex on both sides of the Sierra Nevada range. The dates range from 1770 B.C. to 950 B.C., covering the period of intensive occupation by the Martis peoples.

The projectile point artifacts associated with the North
Fork petroglyphs seem to be mostly for use with the spear or
dart, and prior to introduction of the bow and arrow; they are
strikingly similar to Martis points, and conform to some of the
types seen in the Early Central California points, believed to
date to some 5000-3000 years ago, or the Middle Central
California phase of 4000-1600 years ago. The less certain dating
of the rock carvings by petroglyph style [1000 B.C.-1500 A.D. for
the Great Basin Curvilinear Abstract style] would fit into these
other bits of evidence on the age of the North Fork petroglyphs.

Attempts to classify the symbols in order to infer some
meaning to them for the most part have not been fruitful. Perhaps
the interpretation of the most common and more easily
identifiable symbols, the "rake" and the "bear paw", offers a
very limited explanation of what the carvings may mean. It is
likely that many symbols on the petroglyphs reflect the moiety
and family totems of the hunters. The petroglyphs must have been
primarily for a religious or magic purpose, and not as mere
"doodles".

Suggestive evidence points toward the presence of perhaps
three shamans at the major Indian campground near the site of the
old Summit Soda Springs Hotel [Site #27]. That puberty or
fertility rites were performed there is also suggested. At the
broad rocky platform at Site #22 overlooking the river and the
North Fork hunting grounds, an important shaman ceremonial to
bring success to the hunters on the network of hunting trails is
made evident by the several well-done trail maps incised into the
rock there.

APPENDIX A

Recording the North Fork Petroglyphs

Each symbol or glyph that could be discerned was sketched on graph paper at a scale of 1:10. Photographs were taken of a number of the carvings. They were never "highlighted" by the use of chalk markings, but only natural sunlight was used; water sprinkled on the symbols proved of help in bringing out the carvings at a few sites.

When a sketch is employed, it will quite obviously reflect the person's own interpretation of what he sees. When a photograph is taken, it will be showing what is actually there to be seen under those light conditions. But when a symbol is chalked in before photographing, the chalking again will be the person's own interpretation of what he sees, and the picture will then imply to the viewer that this is actually there and in that form--and this may be most misleading.

A great many of the symbols are so shallow and weathered so badly that they photograph poorly; indeed, they may have to be viewed from an unusual angle or with the sun at a specific angle, with time of day frequently being important for discerning or viewing a petroglyph. A photograph is an excellent way to confirm a sketch, or the size of a carving, but it is dangerous to use it to bring out the detail of a symbol if it is chalked.

There is a good discussion of "recording technicalities" and their hazards in the book by Martineau [19, pp. 188-194].

The location of a petroglyph site was noted by compass triangulation to the major mountain peaks viewed from the site. The altitude was determined through use of an altimeter accurate to 40 feet, and estimate to within 20 feet of the elevation was possible. This permitted marking the location quite accurately on a detailed "7.5 minute"" contour map of the area. General descriptions of the rock itself and of the area around the site were always recorded.

APPENDIX B

The North Fork Petroglyphs in Detailed Sketches

Note: All of these hand sketches have been made by the author to approximate scale, using a 1:10 reduction. Specific details of location and triangulation of the site by compass directions have been left out in these Appendix pages.

Why aren't more specific and helpful directions to a site included? Shamefully, because so many of those enjoying the beauty of the mountains and wilderness don't care whether others to follow may have the same enjoyment, and have no respect for private property. They are vandals, and they can and do desecrate priceless works that are part of our prehistoric past. A sorrowful example: in 1979 I recorded and photographed the striking petroglyphs by Wabena [Site # 2]. Over time, the rock panel had broken into a number of sections. In 1981, two of the rock sections containing carvings were taken away by insensitive vandals. Site # 2 is unprotected. All of the glyphs in the Appendix [p. 93] are recorded here on paper, but sadly all are no longer there on the bedrock of the ridge, with its awe-inspiring vista that the prehistoric Indians enjoyed, but which man-the-vandal now thoughtlessly and uncaringly is destroying.

In the sketches to follow, the dark basalt areas associated with a carving are shown by blacking out the area. Where the granite crust has been broken off or eroded away,, thus eliminating part of the rock carving, a fine dotted line appears in the drawing.

The symbols as shown are _not_ in their natural groupings with respect to each other.

SITE #1. The site includes at least seven
individual locations with petroglyphs, granite
outcroppings encompassing several acres. Good
view to the east and Donner Lake.

├─10 in.─┤

Rock Edge

SITE # 1.   (Continued)

SITE # 1.   (Continued)

SITE # 1.   (Continued)

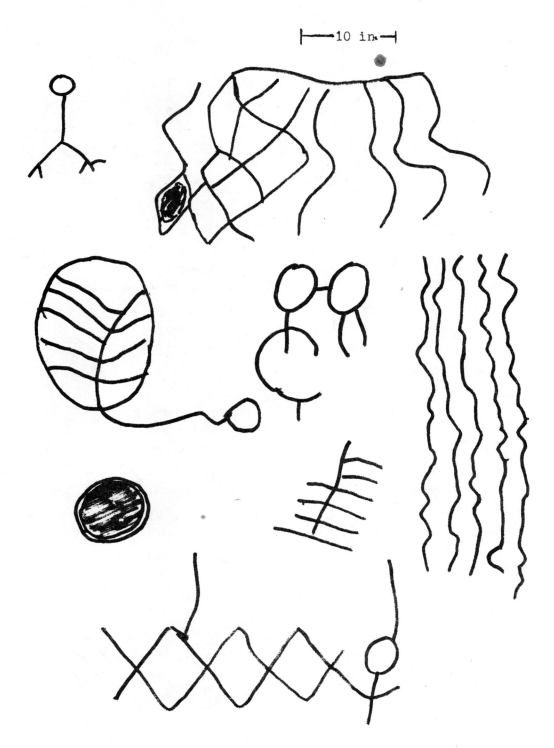

SITE # 1.   (Continued)

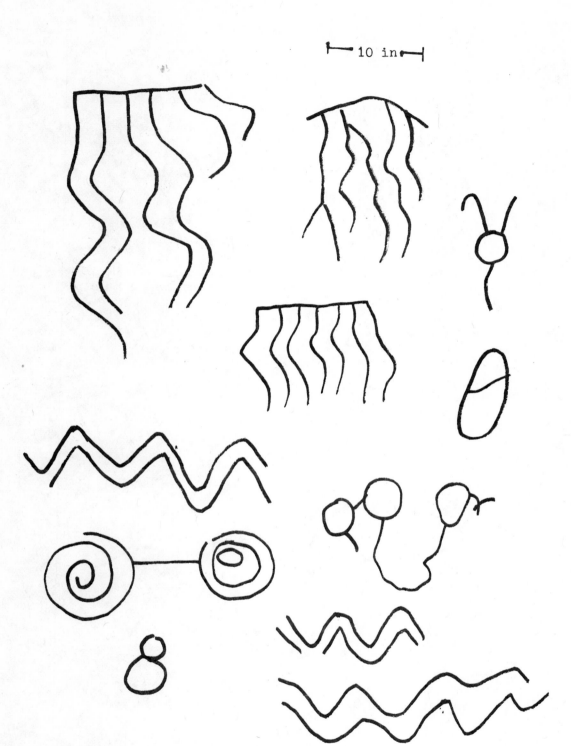

SITE # 1.   (Continued)

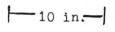

SITE # 1.   (Continued)

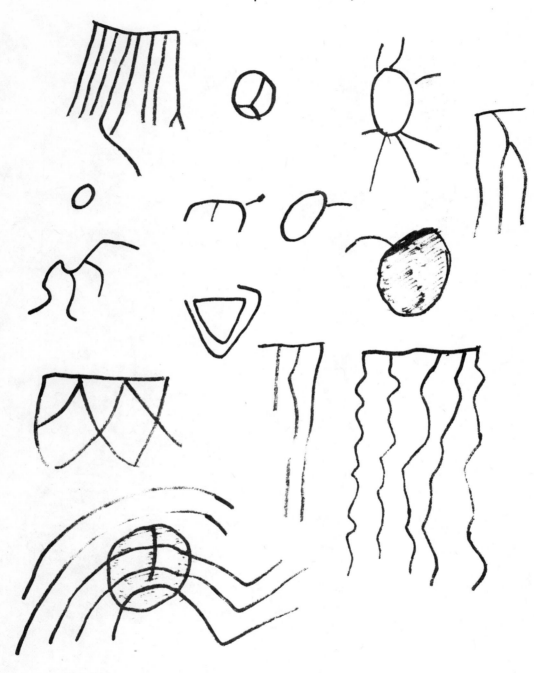

SITE # 1.   (Continued)

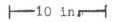
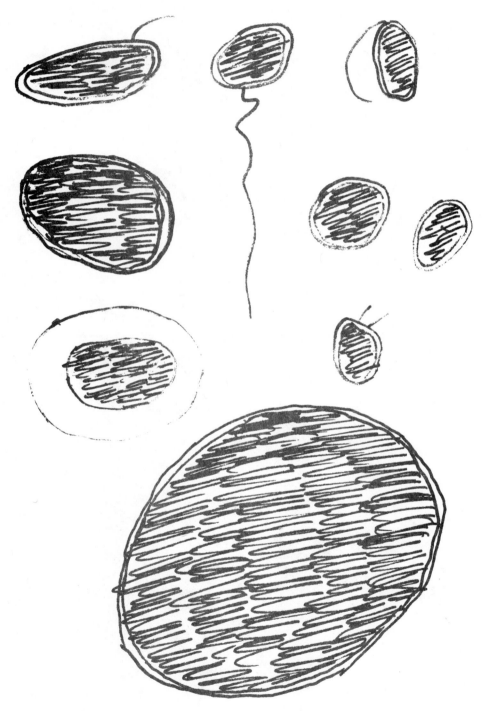

SITE # 1.   (Continued)

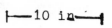

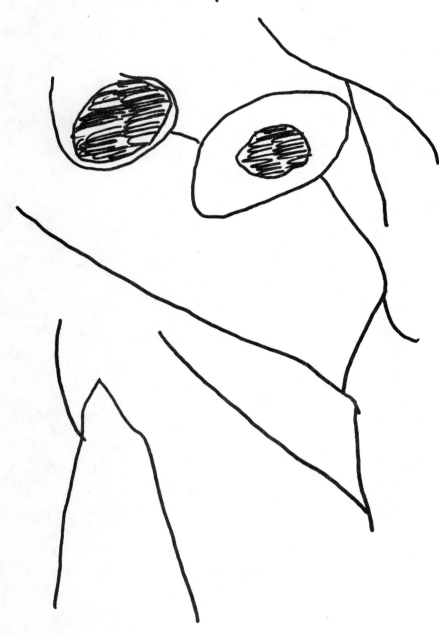

SITE # 1.   (Continued)

┠─10 in─┨

SITE #2. Only a single flat rock suitable for petroglyphs, on a narrow ridge overlooking the Royal Gorge. Carvings relatively deep. Panoramic view of Snow Mt., Devils Pk., Lyon Pk.

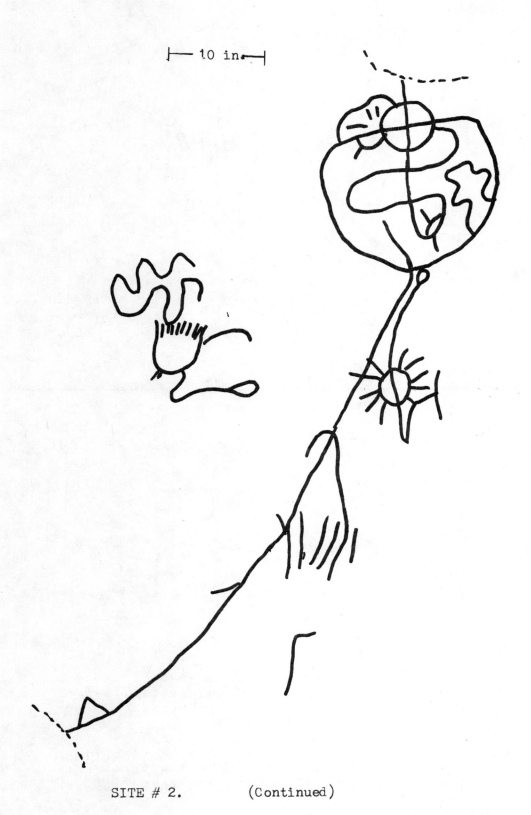

— 10 in. —

SITE # 2.   (Continued)

├─10 in─┤

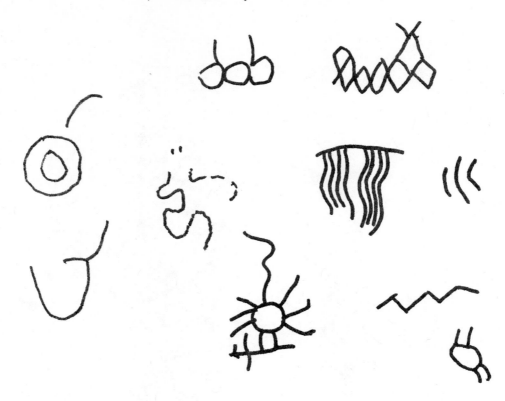

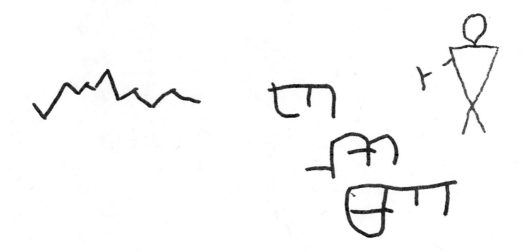

SITE #3 (Top). A rounded glaciated rock nearly crust-free, at a high point. View of Devils Pk., Anderson Pk., Tinkers Knob, Lyon Pk.

SITE #4 (Below). Two rock outcroppings about 30 ft. apart. Sweeping view from near Snow Mt. around to Lyon Pk., and including the dars camp and meadow.

SITE # 5. Three separate rock outcroppings about 50 yds. from each other. Excellent views of Crows Nest, Anderson Pk.,Tinkers
Knob, Lyon Pk.

SITE # 5.   (Continued)

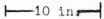
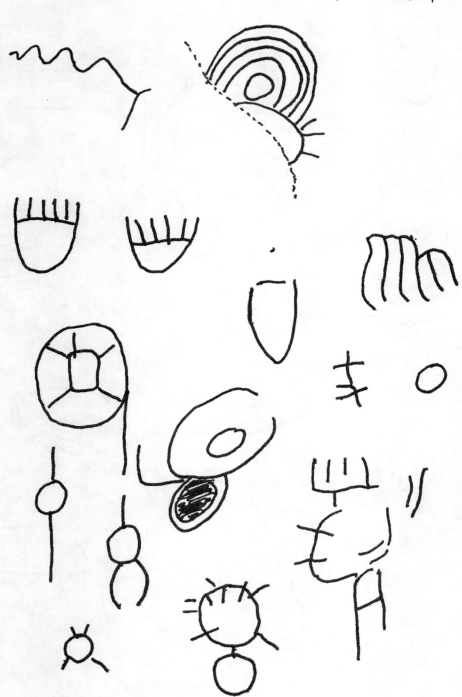

SITE #6. Two long outcroppings, perhaps 50 yds. from each other. View includes Tinkers Knob, Anderson Pk.

├─ 10 in. ─┤

SITE # 6.   (Continued)

100

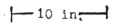

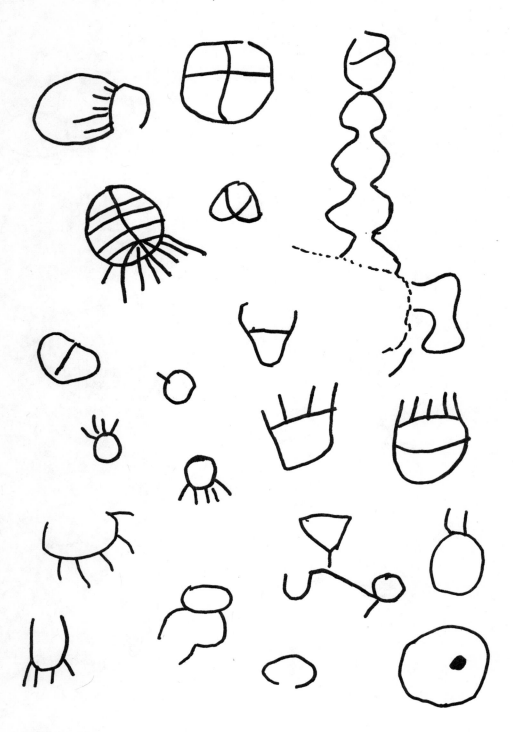

SITE # 6.   (Continued)

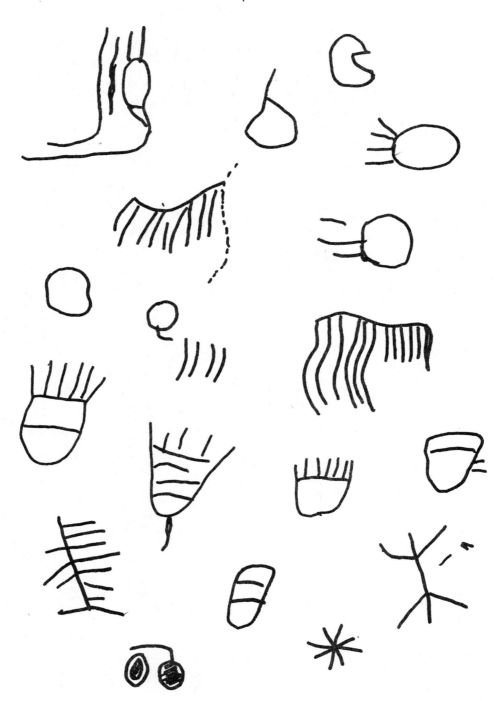

├─ 10 in. ─┤

SITE # 6.   (Continued)

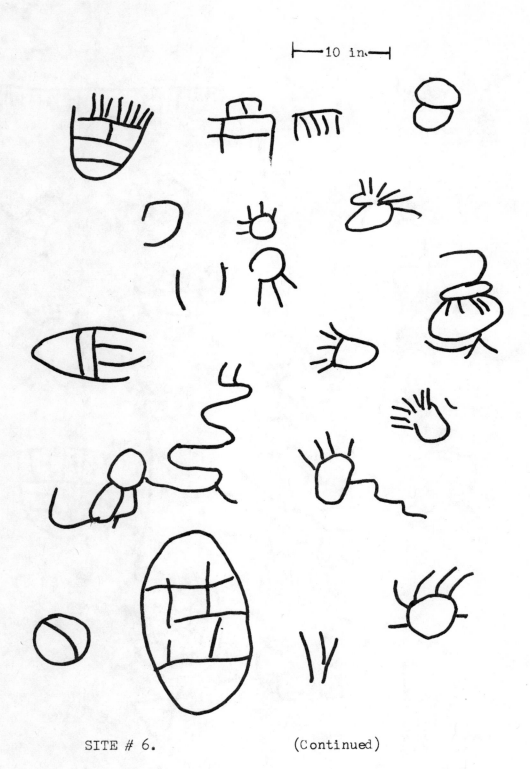

SITE # 6.   (Continued)

├─10 in.─┤

SITE # 6.   (Continued)

—10 in.—

SITE # 6.   (Continued)

├──10 in──┤

SITE # 6.   (Continued)

SITE # 6.   (Continued)

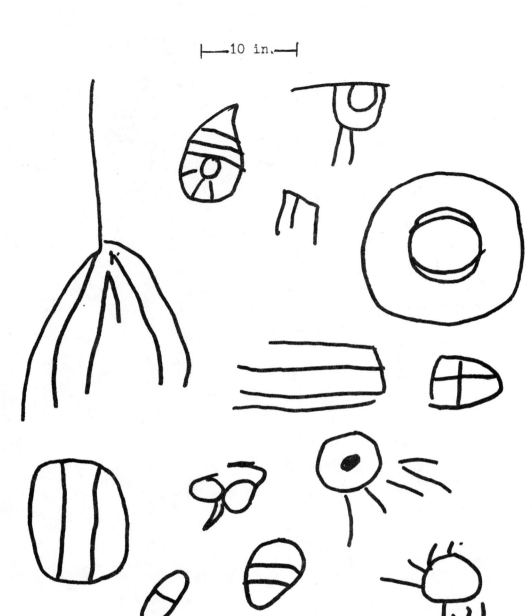

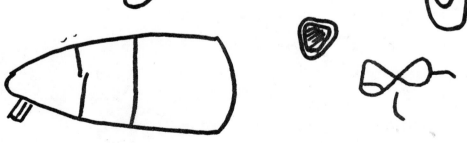

SITE # 6.   (Continued)

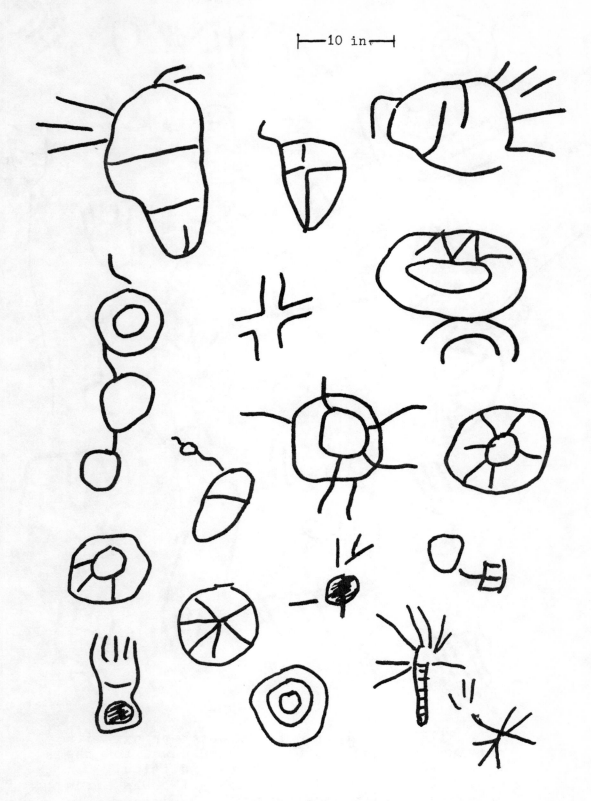

SITE # 6.　　　　　　　　　　　(Continued)

SITE #7. Part of the outcropping with carvings is quite steep, going down to the river. Glyphs are badly worn, difficult to decipher for recording. Views of peaks from just above the petroglyphs.

110

SITE # 7.   (Continued)

SITE # 7.   (Continued)

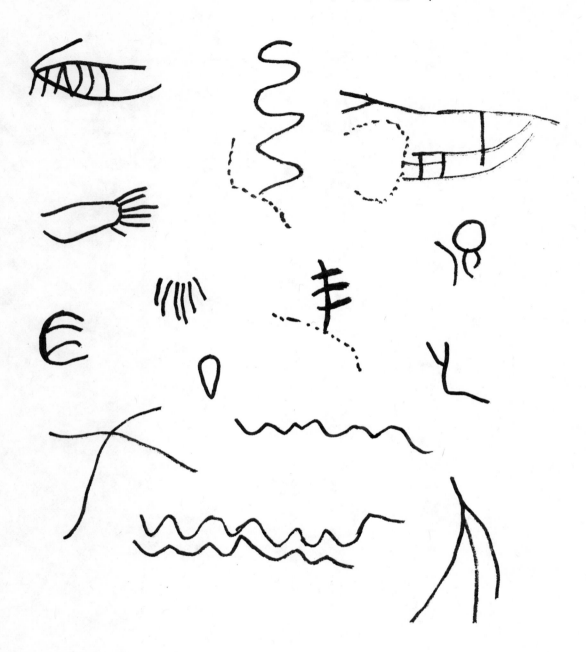

SITE # 7.   (Continued)

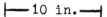

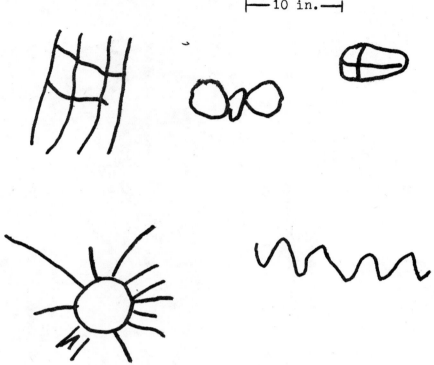

SITE #8. The outcropping has a view of
Tinkers Knob, Lyon Pk. A small heap of flaked
stones by a crevass at the edge of the rock
indicated that a prehistoric artifact maker
had used the rock as a work place.

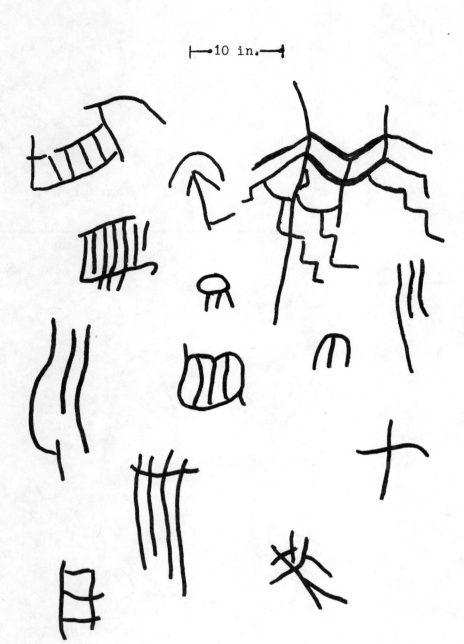

SITE #9. On a rocky dome overlooking the
North Fork, with a 360° vista of all major
peaks.

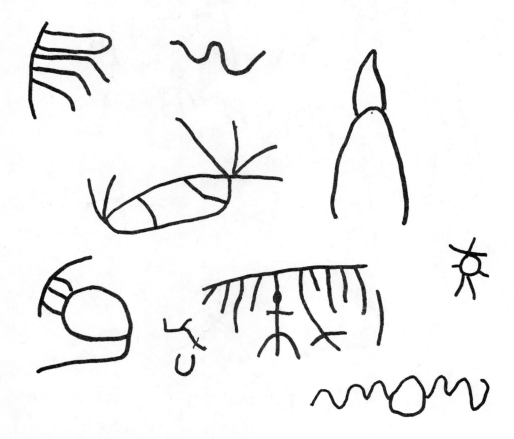

SITE #10 (Top). A roughly square outcropping near the Old Indian Trail, with a view of Anderson Pk., Tinkers Knob.

SITE #11 (Below). On the way up to the major rocky ridge above the river. Three separate locations about 100 yds. from each other on a rocky hill. Views of Snow Mt., Lyon Pk., Tinkers Knob, Anderson Pk.

116

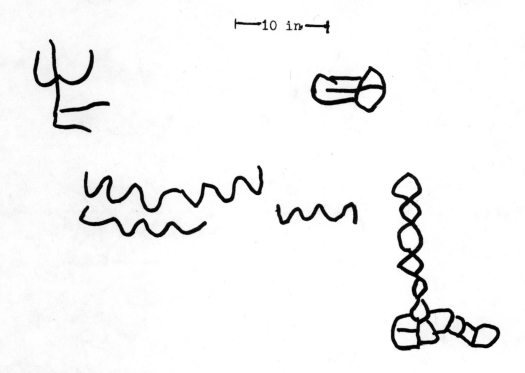

    SITE #12 (Top). A small table area, a
ledge below a rounded top. Views of Snow Mt.,
Devils Pk., Lyon Pk.

    SITE #13 (Below). A small rock outcrop-
ping near a surveyor boundary mark. Major peak
view.

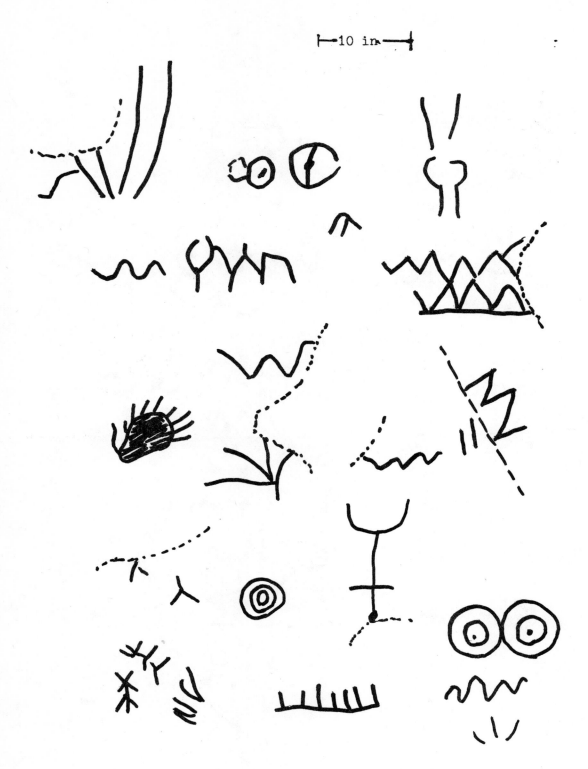

SITE #14. A summit covering many acres of granite outcroppings. Eleven of these had petroglyphs. Views of Snow Mt., Devils Pk., Tinkers Knob, Anderson Pk., Lyon Pk. The dashed line is a quartz vein in the granite.

SITE # 14.   (continued)

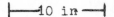

SITE #15 (Top). Two rocky areas, about 100 yds. apart, each with a single glyph. View of Snow Mt., Lyon Pk., Tinkers Knob.

SITE #16 (Below). A large flat granite slope overlooking the upper watershed, with a vista view of Anderson Pk., Tinkers Knob, Lyon Pk., Snow Mt., Devils Pk.

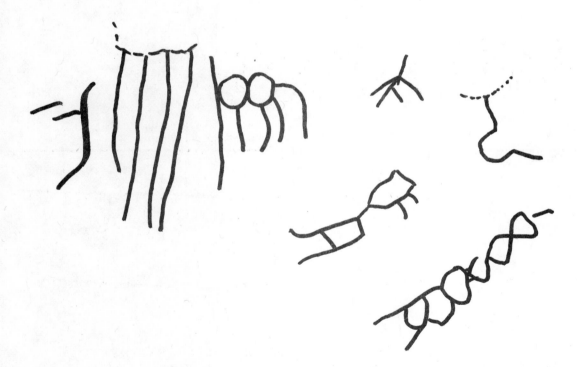

SITE #17 (Top). The outcropping near the
top of a hill and by a gully has views of Snow
Mt., Anderson Pk., Tinkers Knob, Painted Rock.

SITE #18 (Below). This includes three
separate rock outcroppings with views of
Anderson Pk. and Tinkers Knob.

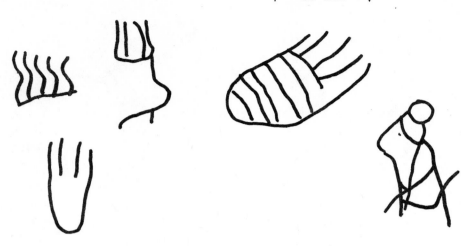

SITE #19 (Top). On the edge of a large
granite rock sloping east. View of Anderson
Pk.

SITE #20 (Middle). Two rocks about 200
yds. south of Site #18.

SITE #21 (Bottom). Faces the mouth of
Lyon Creek, with views of Devils Pk. and Snow
Mt. The "ladder" is 50 yds. away and is
scratched rather than pecked.

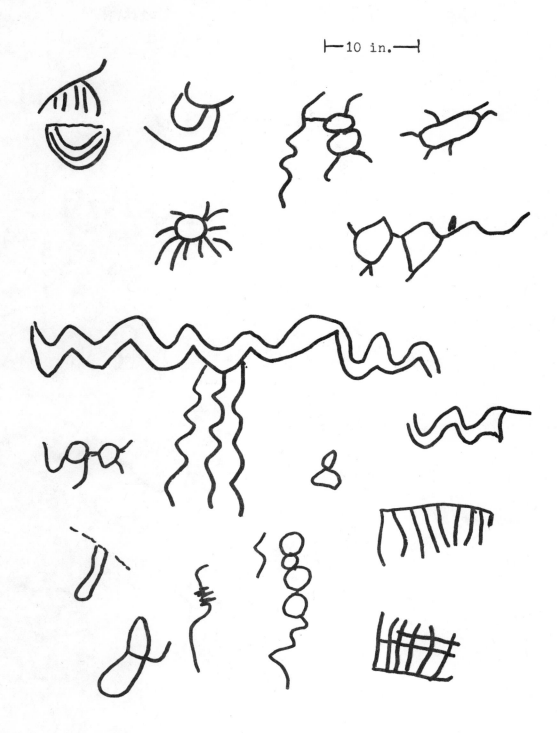

SITE #22. A large granite area with a precipitous drop on the north, plus a smaller outcropping nearby. Well-preserved petroglyphs with views of Anderson Pk. and Tinkers Knob, as well as the upper watershed of the North Fork.

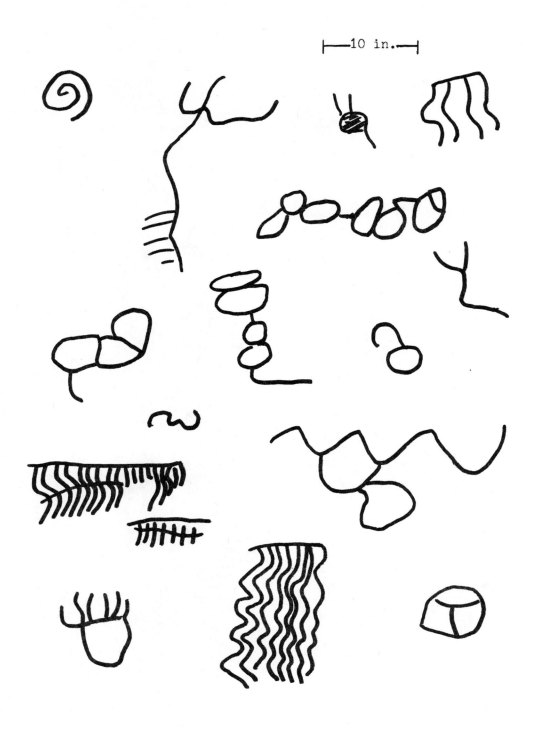

SITE #22.   (Continued)

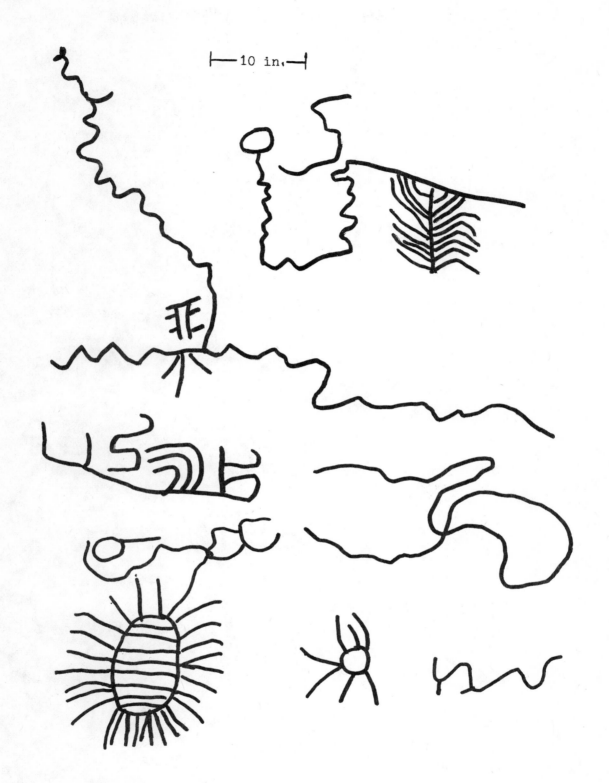

├─ 10 in. ─┤

SITE #22.   (Continued)

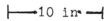

SITE # 22.   (Continued)

SITE # 22.   (Continued)

SITE # 22.   (Continued)

— 10 in. —

SITE # 22.   (Continued)

SITE #23. The major outcropping on a
steep hillside has a slanting ledge, also with
carvings, about 15 ft. lower on the precipitous face. View of Anderson Pk., Tinkers Knob.

├─10 in.─┤

SITE # 23.   (Continued)

131

SITE #24 (Top). A flat granite rock in an area covered with broken boulders. Wide view of peaks from Anderson Pk. to Lyon Pk.

SITE #25 (Middle). A major smooth dome with two glyphs on the east side. View of Snow Mt., Anderson Pk., Tinkers Knob.

SITE #26 (Bottom). A 200 ft. rock dome broken into boulders, but smoothly glaciated on SE side where the glyphs are carved. View of Snow Mt., Anderson Pk., Tinkers Knob.

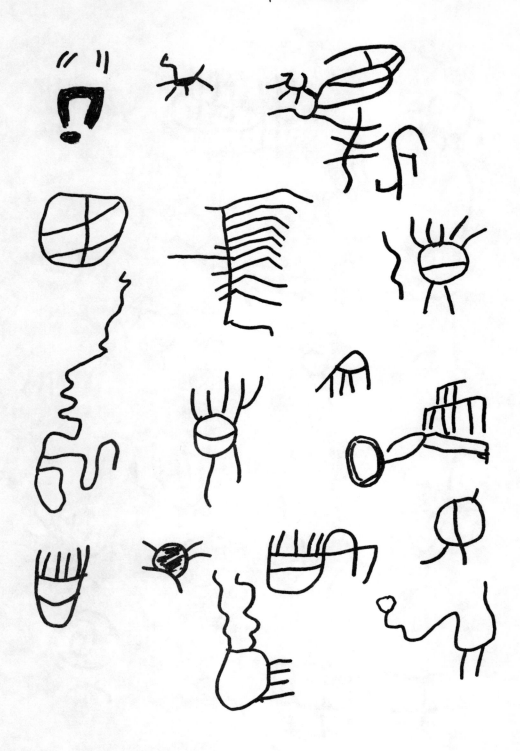

SITE #27. A long sloping rock near the
river and a short distance from the old
Summit-Soda Springs Hotel location. View of
Anderson Pk. and Tinkers Knob.

133

—10 in.—

SITE # 27.   (Continued)

134

├─ 10 in. ─┤

SITE # 27.   (Continued)

135

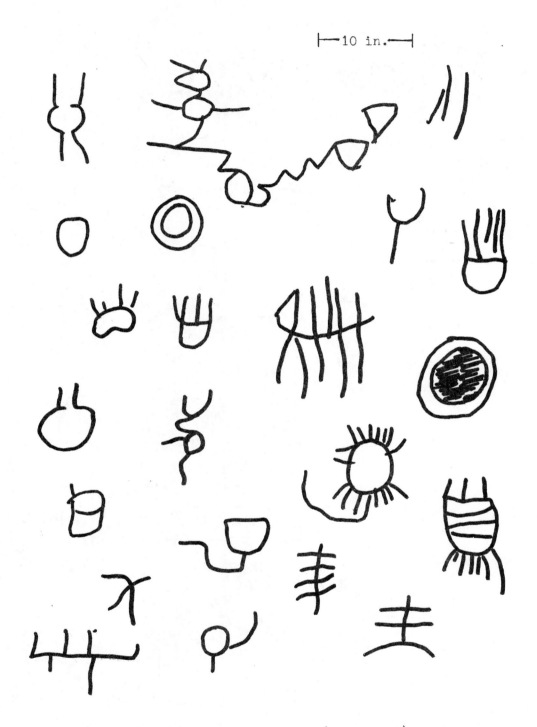

—10 in.—

SITE # 27   (Continued)

—10 in.—

SITE # 27.   (Continued)

SITE # 27.   (Continued)

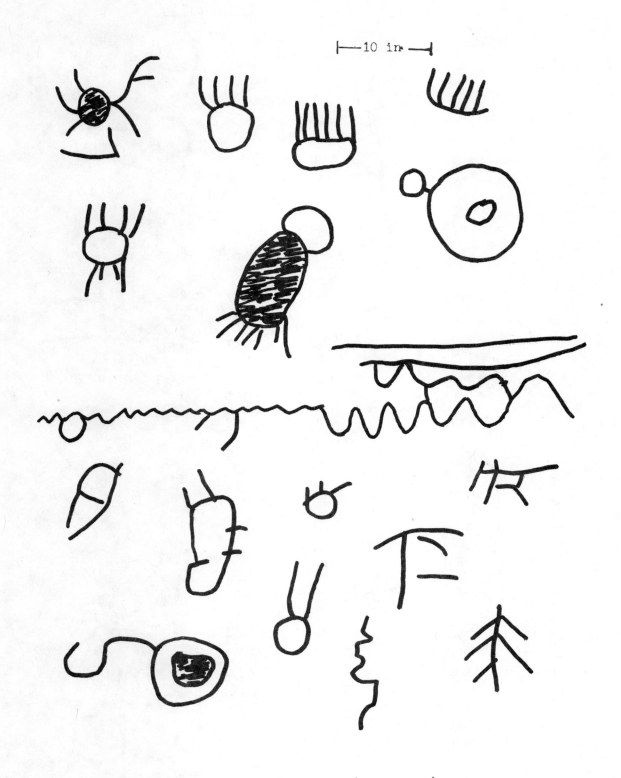

SITE # 27.   (Continued)

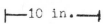

SITE # 27.   (Continued)

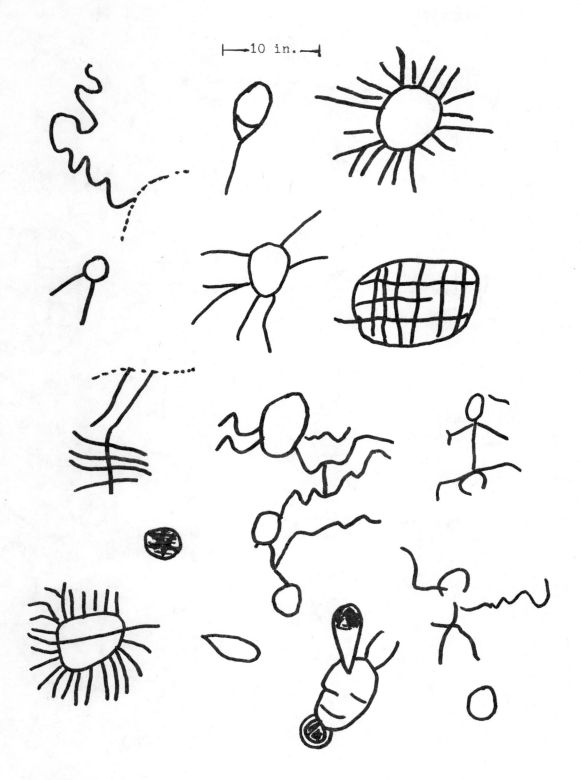

├──10 in.──┤

SITE # 27.   (continued)

SITE # 27   (Continued)

SITE # 27.   (Continued)

SITE # 27. (Continued)

━ 10 in. ━

SITE # 27.   (continued)

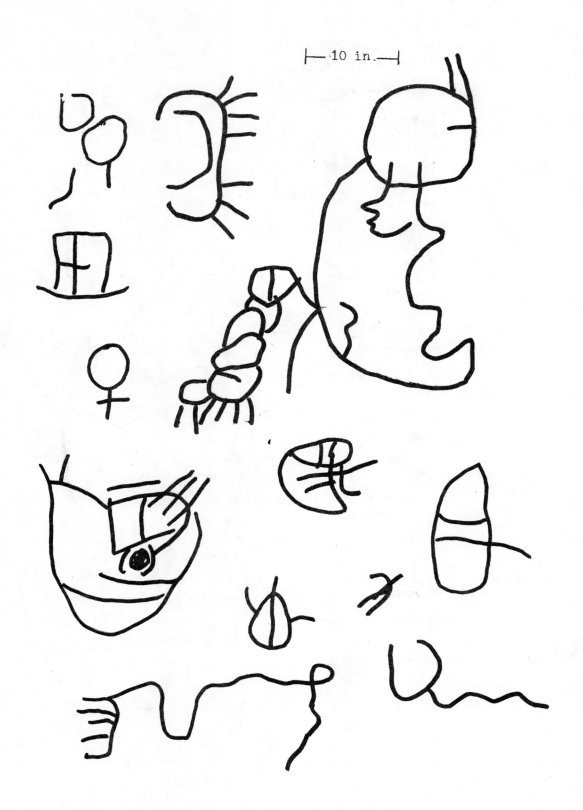

⊢ 10 in. ⊣

SITE # 27.   (Continued)

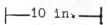

SITE # 27.   (Continued)

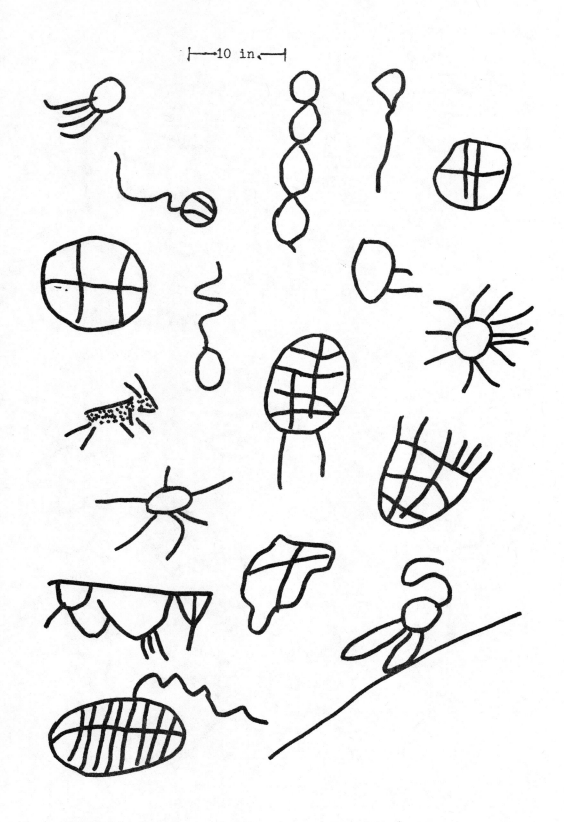

SITE # 27.   (Continued)

SITE # 27.   (Continued)

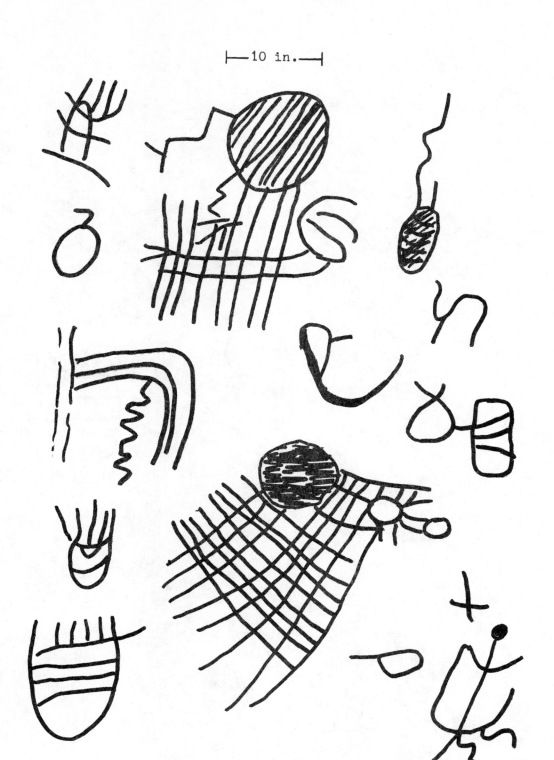

SITE # 27.   (Continued). A white quartz
vein marks the edge of the rainbow-like glyph at the
middle-left.

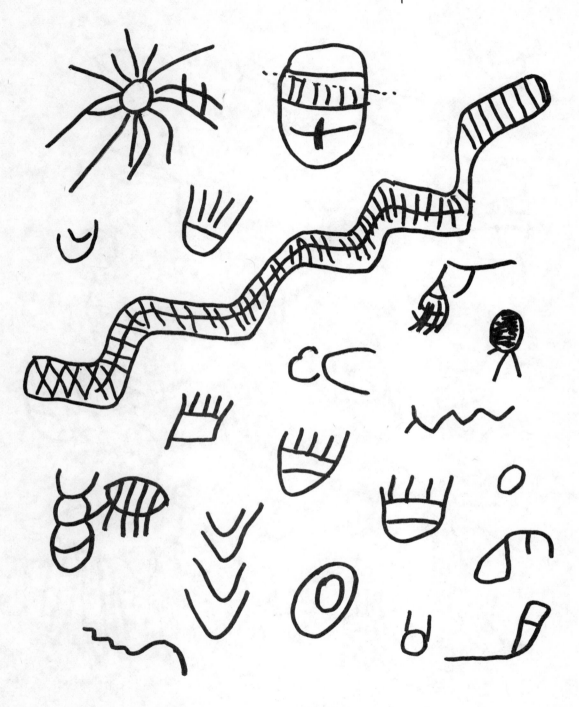

SITE # 27   (Continued)

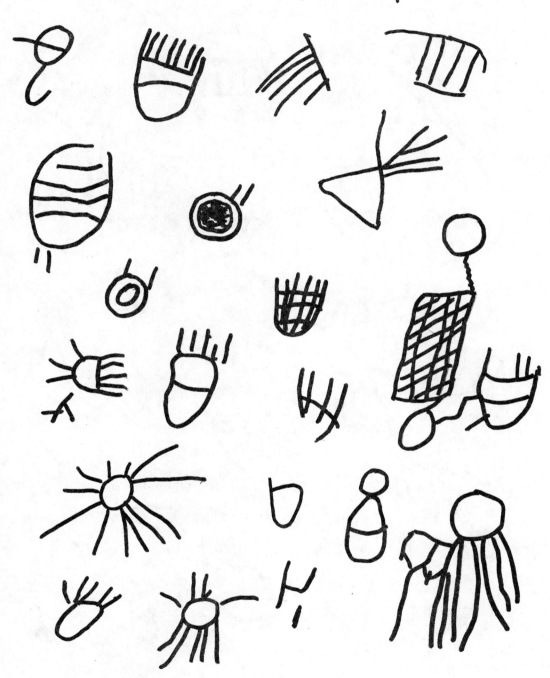

SITE # 27.   (Continued)

SITE # 27.   (Continued)

SITE # 27.   (Continued)

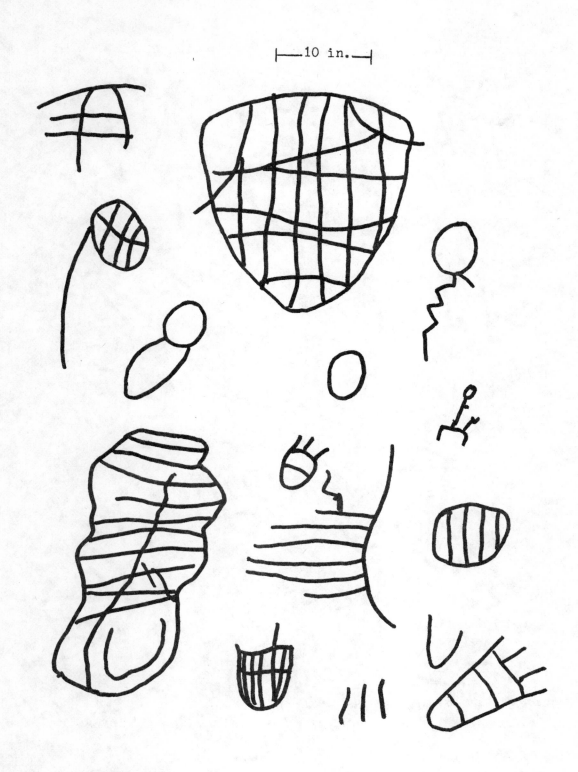

— 10 in. —

SITE # 27.   (Continued)

—|10 in.|—

SITE # 27.   (Continued)

156

SITE # 27.   (Continued)

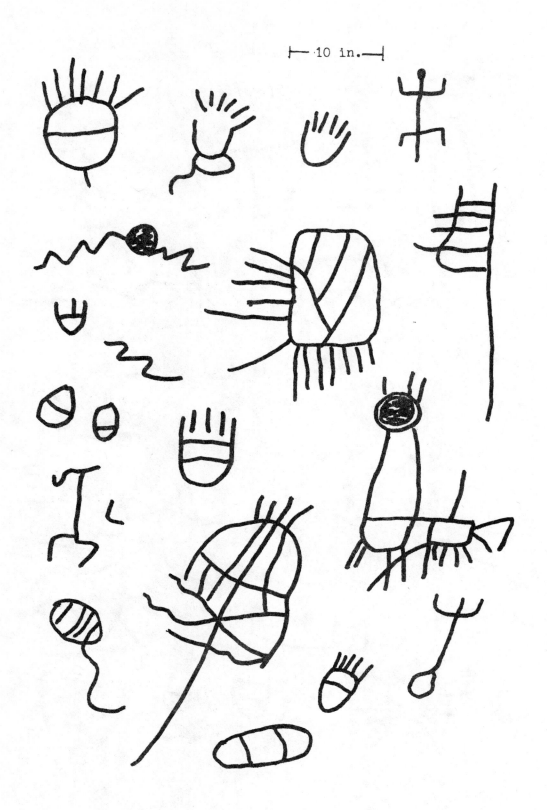

SITE # 27.   (Continued)

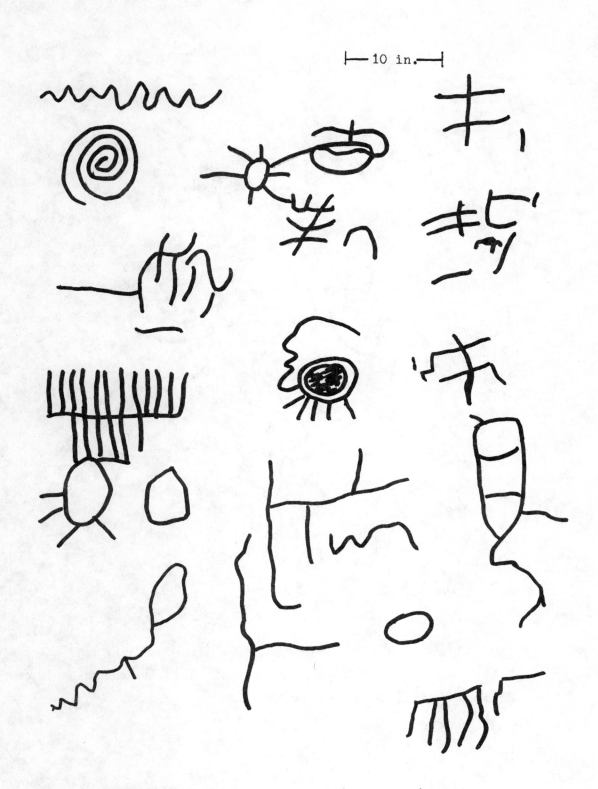

├─ 10 in. ─┤

SITE # 27.   (Continued)

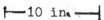

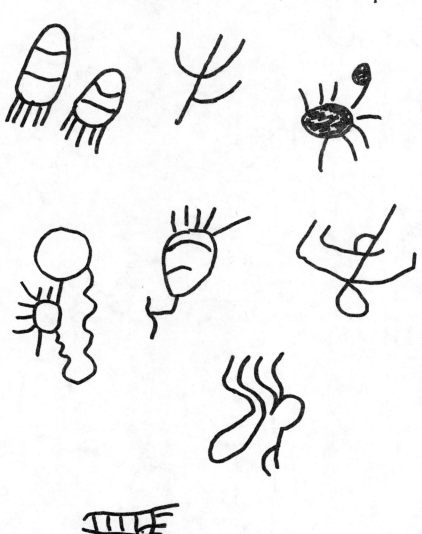

SITE # 27.   (Continued). The "paw" at the
bottom is carved in a basaltic intrusion and is the sole glyph
on a separate rocky area furthest East at this site.

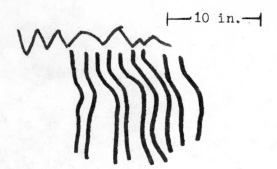

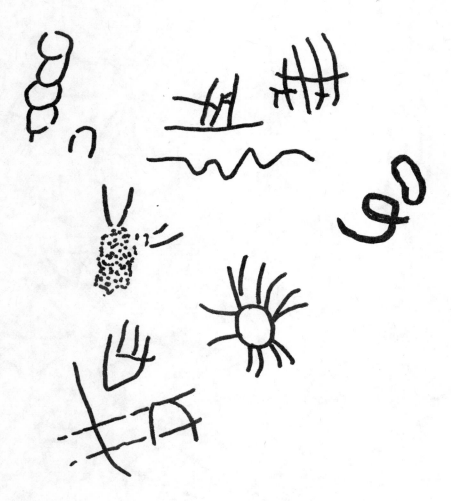

SITE #28 (Top). A small outcropping over-
looking a flat rocky shelf by the Old Indian
Trail. The glyph is in a basalt intrusion.
Views of Snow Mt., Anderson Pk.

SITE #29 (Below). All symbols are pecked
in dark grey basalt intrusions in the granite
outcropping. View of Anderson Pk., Tinkers
Knob.

SITE #30. On the high points of two large granite outcroppings about 150 yds. apart and near the river. View of Anderson Pk.

SITE #31 (Top). The highest of a set of
outcroppings bordering the river, with a view
of Devils Pk. and Anderson Pk.

SITE #32 (Below). The undulating glyphs
are on a granite slope on the west side of the
valley. View of Tinkers Knob. The upper glyph
is in a basalt intrusion in the granite. The
symbol at bottom-right is scraped an inch wide
and is on a flat rock by the creek several
hundred yards further up the valley.

├─10 in.─┤

SITE #33. On sloping granite at the top of the steep trail leading to Mt. Meadow Lake. View of Devils Pk., Tinkers Knob. The bottom three glyphs are on the opposite side of the rock face and in darkened rock rather than the pink-surfaced granite of the others.

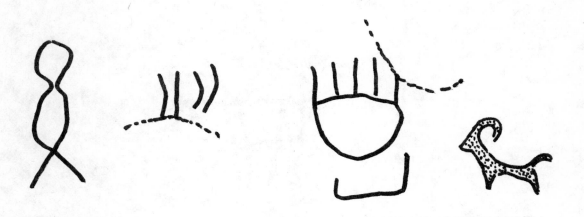

SITE #34 (Top). On one outcropping of many forming a rocky dome of several acres above Inspiration Point. Views of Devils Pk., Snow Mt., Lyon Pk., Tinkers Knob, Anderson Pk.

SITE #35 (Middle). Four separate carvings spaced over the lower 45-50 ft. of the hill rising up toward the rocky ridge from the river. The ram is pecked solid. View of Lyon Peak.

SITE #36 (Bottom). By the sheer drop to the river, below a major granite slope. View of Lyon Pk., Tinkers Knob.

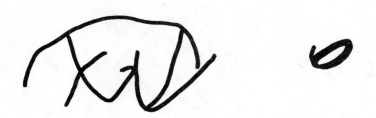

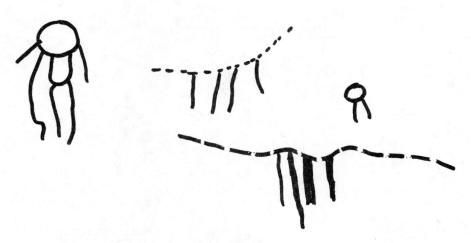

SITE #37 (Top). Near a 30 ft. draw, with views of Anderson Pk., Crows Nest, Lyon Pk.

SITE #38 (Middle). A badly creased and cracked rock dome, with a single carving near the crest. View of Tinkers Knob, Anderson Pk.

SITE #39 (Bottom). Faces the Old Indian Trail, and on a flat top of granite outcropping dropping steeply on the north. View of Anderson Pk., Tinkers Knob. The dashed line represents a quartz vein.

SITE #40 (Top). A single glyph on a large open slope. View of Anderson Pk., Tinkers Knob.

SITE #41 (Below). On a rocky face below a lava crag called Turkey Rock, halfway up the valley.

SITE #42. A long sloping granite
outcropping across the creek below Devils Pk.
View of Snow Mt., Lyon Pk. The dashed lines
are white quartz veins in the granite.

SITE # 42.   (Continued)

├──10 in.──┤

basalt

basalt

SITE # 42.   (Continued)

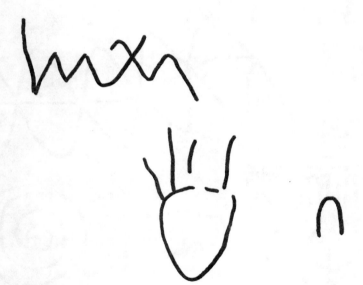

SITE   #43   (Top).   A   high   granite
outcropping west of the peak of Painted Rock
and near a small creek. An undulating rocky
plateau on a steep hillside. Fabulous view of
the North Fork valley.

SITE #44 (Below). Midway up on a rocky
hillside slanting from Granite Creek up toward
north shoulder of Granite Chief. A small
mountain stream is 50 ft. away. View of
Tinkers Knob, Anderson Pk., Needles Pk.

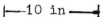

SITE #45. On a finger-like pink granite outcropping at south end of a meadow-swamp going several hundred yards to the north, the East Fork of Palisades Creek. A high rock <u>ca.</u> 50 yds. SW has a view of Snow Mt. and Devils Pk.

SITE # 45.   (Continued)

SITE # 45.   (Continued)

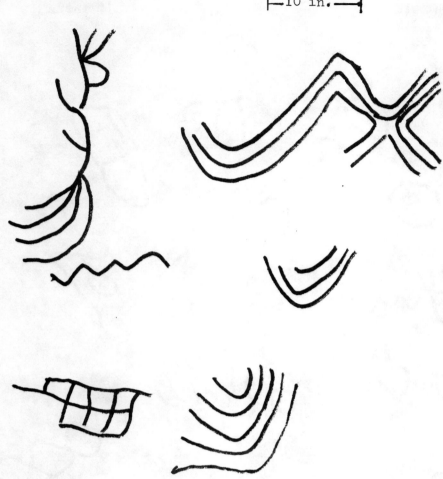

SITE # 45.   (Continued)

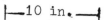

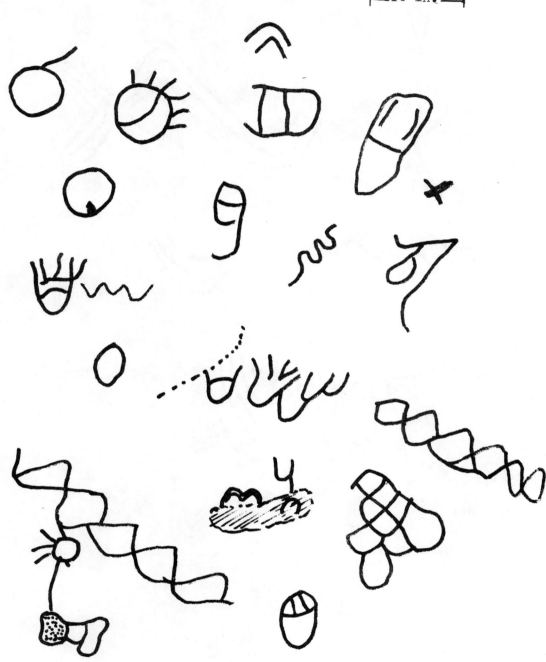

SITE #46. A large volcanic rock rising by
the streambed of the South Fork of the Yuba
River, about a mile west of Cisco Grove along
I-80. The glyphs are mostly in the saddle in
the rock.

SITE # 46.   (Continued)

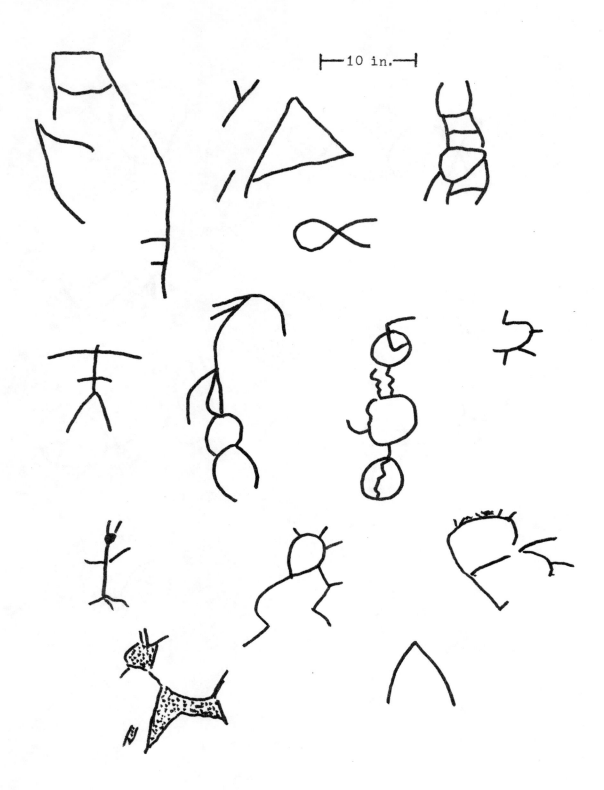

├─10 in.─┤

SITE # 47. Eight individual petroglyph panels on six separate granite outcroppings some hundreds of yards apart. They are on the south and west slopes of a rounded peak rising above the creek. Each panel has a view of one to three mountain peaks, such as Devils Pk., Crows Nest, Anderson Pk., and Lyon Pk.

├─10 in.─┤

SITE # 48. The glyphs are on a flat surface of a
rounded, crusted dome on the northwest slope of
a small peak, and affording a view through the
trees of the road south of the river. Views of
Crows Nest, Anderson Pk., and Tinkers Knob.

PUBLICATIONS CITED

1. Mallery, Garrick. "Picture-Writing of the American Indians." In two volumes. Dover publications, New York. 1972. [Tenth Report of the Bureau of Ethnology. J.W. Powell, Dir., Smithsonian Institution, 1888-89].

2. Heizer, Robert F. and Baumhoff, Martin A. "Prehistoric Rock Art of Nevada and Eastern California." Univ. Calif. Press, Berkeley. 1962.

3. Heizer, Robert F. and Clewlow, C.W. Jr. "Prehistoric Rock Art of California." Ballena Press, Socorro, N. Mex. 1978.

4. Heizer, Robert F. and Whipple, M.A., Eds. "The California Indians: A Source Book." Univ. Calif. Press, Berkeley. 2nd Ed. 1971.

5. Clewlow, C. William Jr., Ed. "Four Rock Art Studies." Ballena Press, Socorro, N. Mex. 1978.

6. Swanton, John R. "The Indian Tribes of North America." U.S. Bureau of American Ethnology Bull. 145. 1952.

7. Heizer, Robert F., Ed. "Handbook of North American Indians. Vol. 8. California." Smithsonian Institution. 1978.

8. Elston, R.G. "A Contribution to Washo Archaeology." Nevada Archaeological Survey Res. Paper No. 2. Nov. 1971.

9. Wilson, N.L. and Towne, A.H., chapter in Reference 7.

10. Conrotto, Eugene L. "Miwok Means People." Valley Publishers, Fresno, CA. 1973.

11. Ritter, Eric W. and Matson, R.G. "Form Categories, Cluster Analysis and Multidimensional Scaling: A Case Study of Projectile Points." Southwestern Lore 37:102. 1972.

12. Jennings, Jesse D. "Prehistory of North America." 2nd Ed. McGraw-Hill Book Co., New York. 1974.

13. Macgowan, R. "Early Man in the New World." Macmillan Co., New York. 1953.

14. Hester, T.R. and Heizer, Robert F. "Review and Discussion of Great Basin Projectile Points: Forms and Chronology." Univ. Calif. Archaeological Res. Facility. 1973.

15. Elsasser, Albert B. "The Archaeology of the Sierra Nevada in California and Nevada." Univ. Calif. Archaeological Survey Rept. No. 51. 1960.

16. Martin, P.S., Quimby, G.F., and Collier, D. "Indians Before Columbus." Univ. Chicago Press, Chicago. 1947.

17. Heizer, Robert F. and Elsasser, Albert B. "Some Archaeological Sites and Cultures of the Central Sierra Nevada." Univ. Calif. Archaeological Survey Rept. No. 21. 1953.

18. Steward, J.H. "Petroglyphs of California and Adjoining States." Univ. Calif. Public. in Am. Archaeology and Ethnology, Vol. 24, No. 2. 1929.

19. Martineau, LaVan. "The Rocks Begin to Speak." K.C. Publications, Las Vegas, Nev. 1973.

20. Grant, Campbell. "Rock Art of the American Indians." T.Y. Crowell Co., New York. 1967.

21. Hudson, Travis and Underhay, Ernest. "Crystals in the Sky: An Intellectual Odyssey Involving Chumash Astronomy, Cosmology and Rock Art." Ballena Press, Socorro, N. Mex. 1978.

22. Reyna, S.G. "La Cueva de la Pileta." Malaga, Spain. 1958. Translated by Maravillas Gortner, 1980.

23. Elston, R.G., Davis, J.O., Leventhal, A., and Covington, C. "The Archaeology of the Tahoe Reach of the Truckee River." Report to the Tahoe-Truckee Sanitation Agency, June 1977.

24. Payen, L.A. "Prehistoric Rock Art in the Northern Sierra Nevada." M.A. Thesis, Sacramento State College, Calif. 1966.

25. Elston, R.G. "The Archaeology of U.S. 395 Right-of-Way between Stead, Nevada and Hallelujah Junction, California." Archaeol. Survey, Univ. Nev. Reno. Nov. 1979.

26. Hester, T.R. "Chronological Ordering of Great Basin Prehistory." Univ. Calif. Archaeological Res. Facility Contrib. 17, 1973.

27. Gifford, E.W. "Miwok Moieties." Univ. Calif. Publications in Am. Archaeology and Ethnology 12: No. 4. 1916.

28. Fell, Barry. "America B.C. Ancient Settlers in the New World." Times Books, New York. 1976.

29. Fell, Barry. "Saga America". Times Books, New York. 1980.

Arabic writing 53
Archaic stage 15, 20
Arrowheads 1, 13, 18, 20, 26
Artifacts [see Projectile points]
Atlatl 16, 18, 20, 21, 26, 35
Basalt 4, 16, 18, 20, 21, 27,
    32, 34, 35, 68, 76, 77,
    80, 83
Boatstone 21
Boulders 32, 33, 78, 80
Bow and arrow 13, 16, 18, 20,
    26, 79, 81
California Culture 14, 15
Campsites 33, 35, 42-45, 48,
    50-52, 55, 62, 65, 76, 80,
    81
Cedars, The 2, 16-22, 26, 29,
    62
Celtic Ogam 53
Chickerings 16, 20, 21, 29, 31,
    33, 59
Clans 7, 67
Cliffs 32, 33
Coldstream Canyon 79
Cultures 14, 15, 20, 53
Desert varnish 4, 10
Design elements 36, 37, 41-43,
    48, 56, 76
Doodling [see Graffiti]
Early Central CA Culture [Early
    Horizon] 15, 16, 20, 25, 81
Eastman, Roberta 18, 19, 21, 23
Emigrant Canyon 79
Fish, Peter 20, 21, 23
Game trails [see Hunting trails]
Glyphs [see also Design Elements]
    astronomical 56, 57, 67, 73,
        76
    description 3, 31-33, 36-43,
        45, 47, 54, 56, 68, 70-72
    environmental 57, 67, 68, 73,
        76
    fertility 70, 81
    maps [see Maps]
    puberty 70, 81
    recording 80, 82
    styles 13, 14, 25, 36, 76
    superposition 11

tallies 51, 58, 73
wavy 4, 36, 41, 43, 45,
    46, 55, 57, 59, 67, 70,
    71, 73, 76
Gortner, Willis 22, 23
Graffiti 10, 45, 50, 67, 81
Granite, crust 10, 26, 27, 53,
    83
    hardness 4, 27
    pink color 10, 11, 27, 32
Great Basin 2, 6, 10, 26, 57
    cultures 14, 48
    styles 13, 42, 45, 47, 48,
        81
Hall, Winslow 18, 19, 23
Hammerstone 5
Hieroglyph 3
Hunting trails 29, 31, 32, 51,
    59, 62, 65, 78, 80, 81
    ambush 35
Indian tribes 6, 7, 25, 57, 70,
    73
Kings Beach Complex 16, 20, 25
Late Central CA Culture [Late
    Horizon] 16, 20, 25
Maidu Indians [see Nisenan]
Maps 51, 55, 58-65, 78, 80, 81
Martis Complex 6, 12, 15, 16,
    20, 21, 23-26, 43, 55, 62,
    65, 68, 79-81
Midden deposits 12
Middle Central CA Culture
    [Middle Horizon] 12, 15, 16,
    20, 25, 81
Migratory trail 1, 55, 59
Miwok Indians 6-9, 43, 67, 70,
    71, 73, 80
Moieties 7, 8, 58, 67, 68, 76,
    79, 81
Nisenan 6, 7, 9, 12, 43, 57,
    67, 80
North Fork Assn. 2, 29
Obsidian 4, 7, 15, 16, 18, 20,
    21
Paiute Indians 6
Paw, bear 36, 37, 40, 43-45,
    47-49, 56, 67, 68, 70, 73,
    76, 77, 81

Petroglyphs, dating 5, 10-14,
    25, 47, 79
  definition of 3
  manufacture of 4
  pecking tool 4, 5
  styles 1, 13, 14, 25, 36,
    42, 43, 45, 47-49, 53, 79,
    81
  views 32, 33, 50, 78, 80,
    82
  weathering 10
Pinehurst Assn. 21, 23, 29,
    33, 52
Projectile points 1, 5, 12-23,
    25, 26, 29, 33, 35, 53,
    55, 62, 79, 81
Quarry 35, 77
Radiocarbon dating 12, 14, 16,
    25, 26, 79, 80
Rakes 36-38, 43-48, 52, 57,
    58, 70, 71, 73, 76, 81
Rock art [see also Petroglyphs]
    3, 29, 56, 79, 80

Rakes 36-38, 43-48, 52, 57,
    58, 70, 71, 73, 76, 81
Rock Art [see also Petro-
    glyphs] 3, 29, 56, 79,
    80
Royal Gorge 1, 29, 30
Shaman 8, 9, 52, 65, 68-70,
    73, 76, 77, 81
Spear-thrower [see Atlatl]
Summit Soda Springs Hotel 11,
    20, 29, 31, 81
Sun disc 36, 37, 39, 41-44, 47,
    48, 67, 70, 73, 76
Symbols [see Glyphs]
Thunderbirds 73-75
Totems 7, 8, 29, 51, 58. 67,
    68, 71, 73, 76, 77, 79,
    81
Washo Indians 6, 7, 11, 32, 43,
    80
Weathering 10, 27, 45, 78, 82
Wilbur, Ray III 18-21